Wearing Special "PPE" in the Workplace

Wearing Special "PPE" in the Workplace

Wonderful Wisdom of Workplace Safety

L. A. Jones

Copyright © 2014 by L. A. Jones.

Library of Congress Control Number: 2014908028
ISBN: Hardcover   978-1-4990-0925-5
               Softcover   978-1-4990-0926-2
               eBook   978-1-4990-0924-8

All rights reserved. No part of this book may be reproduced or transmitted in any form or by any means, electronic or mechanical, including photocopying, recording, or by any information storage and retrieval system, without permission in writing from the copyright owner.

Any people depicted in stock imagery provided by Thinkstock are models, and such images are being used for illustrative purposes only.
Certain stock imagery © Thinkstock.

This book was printed in the United States of America.

Rev. date: 05/05/2014

To order additional copies of this book, contact:
Xlibris LLC
1-888-795-4274
www.Xlibris.com
Orders@Xlibris.com
622987

Contents

Introduction: The Visionary: Seeing Seven Laws of Safety 7

1 Wearing an H.A.R.D. Hat, Not a Hard Head! 11

2 Wearing E.Y.E. Protection: Value Your Vision! 42

3 Wearing E.A.R. Protection: Have Your Hearing! 69

4 Wearing "Wisdom Gloves": Handle Safety Matters Wisely! 97

5 Wearing S.T.E.E.L. Toe Boots: Walk in Wisdom! 125

6 Wearing "Work Clothes" of Common Sense: Use 100% of It! 153

7 Wearing a "Shield": Trust in God as Your Personal Protection! 180

Epilogue: My Seven Year Itch 206

Introduction

The Visionary: Seeing Seven Laws of Safety

One of steel mills' most diligent efforts to keeping their workers safe is providing them with P.P.E., which stands for personal protective equipment.

Personal protective equipment, as found in steel mills, consists of seven basic items which each worker must have . . . and must *wear*.

1. You must wear *a hard hat*.
2. You must wear *eye protection*.
3. You must wear *ear protection*.
4. You must wear *gloves*.
5. You must wear *steel toe boots*.
6. You must wear *work clothes that are 100% cotton*.
7. You must wear *a shield . . . when cutting, wielding, etc.*

When you're *working*, you must be *wearing* these . . . for your safety.
Your safety is the company's highest concern.
To not wear them is to be considered *unsafe*.
But even with all this personal protective equipment, people still get hurt . . . or killed.

> *Where there is no VISION, the people perish: but he that keepeth THE LAW, happy is he.*
>
> —PROVERBS 29:18

Here, the word "vision" has the Hebrew translation of *revelation*.
Revelation is something that is revealed.
Something that is revealed isn't previously known or realized.
A book is a printed work that presents knowledge.
In this book, I share with you *revelation knowledge* behind these seven basic items of personal protective equipment.
Seeing [or realizing] seven laws of safety, I want you to know them and abide by them in the workplace. Each chapter is a solid, powerful discussion of each of these safety laws I discovered.
I genuinely believe that if you keep these seven laws of safety, you will be happy you did!

It is also my genuine belief that where there is no revelation . . . or something revealed to workers in the workplace which they didn't previously know or realize . . . *people will get hurt or killed.*

✴ *What you don't know can hurt or kill you . . . in the workplace!*

I genuinely believe that *wisdom* is the missing key to building and establishing a safe workplace.
A safe workplace consists of *safe workers.*
Safe workers must not only *wear* personal protective equipment. They must also *walk in wisdom* in the workplace.

The company knows and understands that people can be hurt or killed without *knowledge* . . . or specific information about what has the potential to hurt or kill them. So the company continually "schools" its workers on the very important subject of safety.

But I believe the company must go "a second mile" and provide its workers with *wisdom* . . . for them to walk in, while working in the workplace.
Wisdom goes far deeper than knowledge.
▶ Knowledge basically is *information.*
▶ Wisdom invaluably is *insight.*
Workers must not only *know* what specifically has potential to harm them. They must also *understand* the true nature of what they know can harm them and the deeper impact it can have on them.

In this book, I give *special "personal protective equipment"* which you can . . . and most definitely should . . . "wear" in the workplace. I strongly believe it will serve you well, as far as your personal wellbeing goes. You should want to "wear" it simply because you want to do anything and everything to keep yourself from getting hurt . . . or possibly killed . . . in the workplace, where you probably spend most of your time and make your living.

This book presents invaluable insights for the individual worker.

Welcome to Wonderful Wisdom of Workplace Safety for *YOU* to walk in! God Bless . . .

—L. A. Jones

1

Wearing an H.A.R.D. Hat, Not a Hard Head!

● Safety truth:

> *Young workers in the workplace are most prone to be naïve. Wherefore, they should passionately seek to acquire* **prudence, practical information,** *and* **personal discretion**—*marks of mature workers. Mature workers mind their safe conduct.*

Fear is *extreme respect*.

Extreme respect is what you have to have for what has the potential to harm or kill you in the workplace.

What has the potential to harm or kill you in the workplace I call "predators."

Predators have the potential to harm or kill prey.

"Prey" is what people become when they fail to extremely respect what can hurt or kill them in the workplace. They can be daredevils or simply desperate people, who're desperate to get things done.

Fear is for prey!

Machinery and all kinds of operating equipment in the workplace are "predators" which have the potential to harm or kill you. I refer to them as "predators" because they lack the capability of compassion and to care for you. They will simply do what they're designed to do. That's exactly where extreme respect for them comes in. You must simply learn to fear them. When I say "Fear them," that's exactly what I mean! You must have a *GENUINE FEAR* for these very things. They render the very areas wherein they're found *VERY DANGEROUS!* That's why these dangerous areas (of the workplace) are considered "restricted areas." Restricted areas can only be entered by authorized personnel, for Safety's sake.

Using the word *HARD* as an acronym, I let each letter stand for the following:

Healthy
Awesome
Respect (for the)
Dangerous

You need to have a healthy, awesome respect for the dangerous . . . or what can harm or possibly kill you. Without it, you'll be a hardheaded worker! You will be stubborn or unreasonably unyielding to the company's demand for safe practices and safe performance in the workplace.

A healthy, awesome respect for the dangerous is *a choice.*
More specifically, it is a *personal choice.*
It is a personal choice which has to be made *continually.*
It has to be made continually because you will be tempted.
You will be tempted to *take shortcuts.*

B.E.E. Sting!

● Safety truth:

> *A wise worker will **listen** and therefore will **learn** how to be safe in other areas of concern. Humility is the key to higher learning.*

Using the word *BEE* as an acronym, I let each letter stand for the following:

Beware (of)
Envying
Employees

You have to be careful to not envy employees who *take chances . . . with their personal wellbeing and even with their very life*.

Don't envy them . . . no matter their veteran experience and value to their superiors and the company.

Don't try to do every thing they do . . . especially if it's *unsafe*.

What they may consider to be *confidence* may well be *cockiness*.

☞ *Be confident . . . but don't be cocky!*

You just may get "stung" by envying employees who take shortcuts or take shameless risks.

Overconfidence causes you to override any sense of danger or cause for concern.

7 Rewards for Respecting What's Really Dangerous

1. **Respecting what's really dangerous will demonstrate that you're a wise worker.** A wise worker won't be "led astray" by a foolish worker. A wise worker "knows better." He knows and understands the grave importance of being safe. *A wise worker is a safe worker.* You simply cannot deceive him into doing something unsafe.
2. **Respecting what's really dangerous will help you live longer.** *Shortcuts Will Shorten Your Life.* You don't just want to live for that day. You want to live to work another day, and so on.
3. **Respecting what's really dangerous will give you strong confidence.** Strong confidence and overconfidence are not the same. A strongly confident worker is *focused on what he's doing.* An overconfident worker is *blind about what he's doing.*
4. **Respecting what's really dangerous will teach you to hate unsafe acts and unsafe habits.** A safe worker is one who's been *taught* to be safe. Should you get behind in your work, you won't allow desperation to "get caught back up" to prevail upon you. Nor will you try to "show out" in the workplace by attempting dangerous stunts of any kind.
5. **Respecting what's really dangerous will be a "living fountain" to you, to keep you from the "hidden traps" of personal**

injury and unexpected death. A fountain is a *source*. Respecting what's really dangerous will be a source for you that will lead to your continual living.

6. **Respecting what's really dangerous will cause you to "keep your hands clean."** You will avoid unsafe practices that will get you into trouble with the company . . . that's adamant about work safety. The company takes safety violation very seriously.
7. **Respecting what's really dangerous will guide you in discovery of "secrets" or hidden mysteries of danger and safety.** You learn as you live. As you *respect* what's really dangerous, you begin to *realize* things about those dangers . . . and the true spirit of Safety. You become empowered by experience.

Watch Out for "UFOs": Unexpected Flying Objects!

● Safety truth:

> *If an employee doesn't understand the principle of how something works, then he shouldn't attempt to work on it, in hope of **finding out** what's wrong with it and **fixing** it.*

The production process is not a perfect one.

Sometimes, things go wrong in the production process, which can *unexpectedly* send objects flying in the workplace.

If you're *absorbed in* your work, then you won't be *attentive to* what's going on *around you* and you may not see *airborne objects,* as they may come flying your way.

You have to watch out for unexpected flying objects! If you don't, they can catch you off guard!

No matter how well the workplace may be guarded . . . with every guard that can be possibly placed anywhere . . . you have to stay on guard!

↯ *To stay safe, you have to stay alert!*

You have to *watch* while you *work*.
While you work:

- *Look around* from time to time.
- *Listen for* abnormal or unusual sounds, like crashing.
- *Leave where you are* when you see an unexpected flying object in your work area. Get clear of it!
- *Learn* what part of the work area it came from, to report it, to help investigators "figure out" how to prevent a repeat episode.

While you work, don't just use *machines*. Use your *mind!*
Your mind is key to keeping yourself safe.
Keeping yourself safe is a 24-hr job itself.
While you keep at your work, you have to keep at being safe. Just as you may have the ability to walk and chew gum at the same time, you have to have the ability to work and be safe at the same time.

"UFOs" (unexpected flying objects) may have *rare sightings;* nevertheless, they're *real happenings.*
So don't count them out! They must be watched out for, too!
They can cause:
▶ Property damage
▶ Personal injury
▶ Plain death

If you've never seen a "UFO" (unexpected flying object) in the workplace, just know they sometimes do *appear* . . . and at *unexpected times.*
Unexpected times can be times of *unexpected death.*

The Invisible "Hurricane" in the Workplace

● Safety truth:

> The **specific information** the company gives you concerning workplace safety is primarily aimed at raising and retaining your **special respect** for what's harmful . . . to you.

In many incidents in the workplace, which were rightfully reported and thoroughly investigated, upon interrogation, the *majority* of people, who were actually involved, had this common confession: "I became complacent."

As I thought on this "Achilles' heel" of many workers called complacency, what came to my mind was a *hurricane*.
A hurricane is huge.
Complacency is *huge* in the workplace.
It is of exceedingly great extent among workers.

I call complacency the invisible "hurricane" in the workplace.
People fear a hurricane. But a hurricane doesn't do the actual damage. It's the *tornadoes* in a hurricane that cause the actual damage.
▶ It's not the *gun* but the *bullet* that causes the actual damage.
▶ It's not the *bow* but the *arrow* that causes the actual damage.
Complacency doesn't cause the actual damage. It is the "tornadoes" in the "hurricane" of complacency that cause the actual damage.
The "tornadoes" in the "hurricane" of complacency are *losses*.

Complacency leads to:

- Loss of *focus* . . . on what you're doing
- Loss of *awareness* . . . of what's going on around you
- Loss of *concern* . . . for what may happen
- Loss of *memory* . . . of what you're supposed to do
- Loss of *respect* . . . for what can hurt or kill you

Just as it's not that gun that gets you but the bullet fired from that gun . . . just as it's not that bow that gets you but the arrow that's shot from that bow . . . it's not that "big concern" called complacency that gets you but those "little losses" that occur in complacency.

A hurricane is a *storm*.
But it's not the *only kind* of storm there is. There are other kinds of storms.

The world has its weather conditions.
The workplace has its *workers' conditions*.

Workers' conditions of the workplace to which I refer I call "storms." Complacency is just one of these kinds of workers' conditions or "storms."

7 Kinds of "Storms" That Occur in the Workplace

1. **The "storm" of *complacency*.** Complacency is the *condition* of being complacent. Being complacent is being content or self-satisfied coupled with an *unawareness of danger*. When a worker becomes complacent, he finds himself working "in his own little world," which excludes the world immediately around him.
2. **The "storm" of *distraction*.** Distraction is the *condition* of being distracted. A distracted worker is one who's turned away from the original focus of his attention. When he's distracted, he's no longer *paying attention* to what he's doing.
    ▶ Don't let a *conversation* become a distraction.
    ▶ Don't let a *common event* become a distraction.
    ▶ Don't let *confusion* [about something] become a distraction.
    ▶ Don't let your *concentration* [on one thing] become a distraction to you [from another thing].
3. **The "storm" of *anger*.** Anger is the *condition* of being angry. An angry worker is like a drunken person, who cannot "think clearly" or "see straight." His anger "blinds" him. A blind person doesn't "see" what's coming . . . at him or towards him.
4. **The "storm" of *worry*.** Worry is the *condition* of being worried. A worried worker is a troubled person who feels uneasy or concerned about something. *Worry* and *work* can be a dangerous combination. What one worries about holds his attention. His attention then is not on what he's doing . . . or what's going on around him.
5. **The "storm" of *daydreaming*.** Daydreaming is the *condition* of absentmindedly dreaming while awake. The worker's body is in the *actual workplace*; but, his mind is in *another world*. In another world, he doesn't know *what's going on* in the real world . . . what's going on around him. Daydreaming makes him a "sitting duck" for a serious situation.

6. **The "storm" of *proudness*.** Proudness is the *condition* of being proud. When a worker becomes proud . . . for whatever reason . . . he doesn't consider the *friendly suggestions* or *friendly reminders* of others. He thinks himself to be *self-sufficient*. This makes him think also that he doesn't need anyone . . . or anyone's help . . . whether in the form of friendly advice or friendly admonition.
7. **The "storm" of *overzealousness*.** Overzealousness is the *condition* of being overzealous. An overzealous worker is *too anxious* to get something done. This can cause him to fail to see pitfalls ahead of him. While his eyes look straight ahead, avoiding distraction in the process, his head is held up, having his mind on his *mission*. But, he doesn't look low, to see the pitfalls in his path. Because he *knows where he's going* doesn't mean he shouldn't *watch where he's stepping*.

"Storm Watcher"

For that "storms" occur in the workplace, you have to be what I call a "storm watcher."

A storm watcher *watches for storms*.

A "storm watcher" to whom I refer is a *prudent person*.

A prudent person is careful about his conduct.

A "storm watcher" is careful about how he *performs his work*.

He *considers the possibilities* of what may happen in how he performs his work.

Key example:

Let's take, for example, a worker who's "breaking out" a bundle:
He grabs a certain bar that doesn't give.

Key observations:

1. He *sees* that bar doesn't give.
2. He *sees* that bar is trapped because of tremendous weight of other bars lying on top of it.
3. He *sees* he's not strong enough to free that bar.

Key question: What should he not do?

He should not *persist* in trying to free it. He already realizes he's not strong enough to free it. Persistence in trying to free it is *determination*. He should not be determined to free it. It's like a person trying to pick up a car. A car is *too heavy* for a person to pick up. A person can *hurt himself* trying to pick up something that's too heavy *for him*. You can hurt yourself trying to move something that's simply too heavy . . . or too stubborn (won't give)!

Key solutions: What should he do?

1. He should try *another approach* (that's safe) to free that bar.
2. He should *get help* to free that bar.
3. He should simply *leave that bar alone* and reach for another one that's free or possible to safely free.

The "storm watcher" *protects* his self from "storms" and the real damage they can cause.

However, the worker who refuses to watch for "storms" will *suffer for it*.

He will suffer for it because he will be *caught off guard*.
To be caught off guard is to *not be prepared*.
He's not prepared to *meet them*.
He must simply learn to expect the unexpected.

Do You Believe in "Ghosts?"

● Safety truth:

> *Foolish employees **hate** specific information that can **help** them dodge incidents. Wise employees **love** specific information that can **lead** them [safe and sound] through their workday.*

Ghosts aren't *readily seen* before they *really appear*.
What I call "ghosts" in the workplace are *freak accidents*.
Freak accidents occur *without warning*.
They are totally unexpected, unforeseen, and unprepared for.
There's simply no *humanly possible* way to prepare for them. You don't know:

● From what *direction* they may come
● From what *condition* they may happen
● To what *person* they may "appear"

Because you expect the unexpected doesn't mean . . . or guarantee . . . you will see it *in time*.
What you don't see in time you will be *too late to dodge*.
What is too late to dodge will result in either an *injury* or a *fatality*.
Therefore, if anything *looks unsafe, leave it alone!* Have it checked out, to determine if it poses any real danger. Better to be safe than to be sorry.

"Freaky Friday"

Friday is normally the last day of work of a worker's workweek. Work beyond Friday is usually considered overtime.

"Freaky Friday" is what I call a worker's last day of work.
A worker's last day of work can be a time in which the worker's mind is preoccupied with *weekend plans* he's made and mightily excited about.
Weekend plans can "wear away" the worker's *focus* . . . on what he's doing.

When his focus is "worn away" by mental preoccupation of his weekend plans, it may "expose" him to a *fierce incident* . . . or even a *fatality.*

The worker simply must discipline himself to be focused on his "freaky Friday" . . . his last day of work.

His last day of work could very well be his last day to be alive!

L. A.'s Law

I'm fairly certain you've heard of Murphy's Law, which states: "Anything that can go wrong, will go wrong."

I've also discovered a law. I call it *L. A.'s Law.*

L. A.'s Law states: "Potential to harm or kill is always ready to be released."

Whatever has the potential to harm or kill you should always be *respected* . . . because its dangerous potential is always ready to be *released.*

I've witnessed this law in action . . . in the workplace especially . . . countless times.

- ▶ If you don't respect a living, breathing, sizable crocodile, its dangerous potential (to harm or kill) can be released . . . upon you.
- ▶ If you don't respect a living, breathing, very poisonous serpent, its dangerous potential (to harm or kill) can be released . . . upon you.

When you don't *respect* what possesses dangerous potential, it will *result* in your harm.

Your harm can be avoided . . . in many instances.

You can actually:

- *Learn* L. A.'s Law
- *Live by* L. A.'s Law
- *Lengthen* your life by L. A.'s Law

This law is a *law of survival.*

You must seek to survive your workplace . . . and that from day to day.

No one can be safe *for you.*

You have to be safe *for yourself.*

Especially, if you support a household: You cannot take care of your loved ones if you don't take care of yourself . . . in the workplace.

To take care of yourself in the workplace, you have to be safe.

To be safe, you have to respect what can take you out . . . and take you away from your loved ones.

When your loved ones lose you, they lose their *main supporter.*

Losing their main supporter should *matter* to you. It should *mean something* to you.

The "War" in the Workplace: "Warfare Weapons"

◕ Safety truth:

> A **submissive** employee will listen to the **sound** instruction of his **serious** company.

Whether or not you're *aware of* it, there is an ongoing "war" in the workplace.

A war is a state of open, armed, often prolonged conflict carried on between nations.

A war is comprised of *battles.*

The "war" to which I refer is the *War for Safety.*
The War for Safety consists of *safety battles.*
Safety battles are battles to be safe, fought by the workers.
The workers are Safety's *allies.*
There are Safety's *enemies.*

This safety conflict that continues is carried on between the allies of Safety and the enemies of Safety.

The enemies of Safety have their "warfare weapons."
The allies of Safety must have their "warfare weapons," too.
Safety battles are fought on the "battlefield" of the mind.
The mind is where safety begins . . . and must be retained.

"Warfare Weapons" of Safety's Enemies

Here is a list of the "weapons of warfare" employed by Safety's enemies:

1. *Strongholds.* Battles against these take place in *areas of thinking* that are dominated or occupied by the enemy. This is why you can't get some things "through" to some people. Some people will go right to work and commit an unsafe act after having come out of a safety meeting.
2. *Debates.* Battles against these take place in the *area of reasoning.* These are discussions involving opposing points. Some safety offenders try to *argue* their case, to *avoid* getting into trouble. They simply don't "see" anything wrong with what they have done. So they seek to "defend" themselves through these discussions.
3. *High-minded ideas.* Battles against these also take place in the *area of reasoning.* They are conceived by rebellious workers: those who want to do things *their way,* rather than do things *their superior's way.* They arrogantly aim at being their own boss in the workplace; but they will "cooperate" when they see they have no other choice . . . if they don't wish to get into trouble for insubordination.
4. *Rebel thoughts.* Battles against these take place in *areas of thinking.* Workers will think to do wrong . . . to take shortcuts . . . to deliberately commit unsafe acts. The *longer* they think about doing it, the *more* they will want to do it. Rebel thoughts lead to wrong desires. Wrong desires can lead to unsafe acts. Unsafe acts can lead to injuries . . . or fatalities. Unsafe acts are *acts of disobedience.* Acts of disobedience should be readily revenged by the company.

"Warfare Weapons" of Safety's Allies

Here is a list of the "weapons of warfare" employed by Safety's allies:

1. The "weapon" of *correction*. This is punishment intended to rehabilitate or improve. For some workers, who don't seem to "get it," words [including words of warning] may prove to be insufficient. "A servant cannot be corrected by mere words; though he understands, he will not respond," (Proverbs 29:19, NIV). "Strongholds" cannot be demolished by mere words. They require *punishment*. Punishment is *disciplinarian action*. Disciplinarian action is what these workers require.
2. The "weapon" of *reason*. When workers want to debate their safety violations, they have to be reasoned with. They *challenge* on the "battle ground" of reasoning. Those who accept their "challenge" must be patient with them, to give them good understanding, to plainly show them the errors of their ways . . . and the consequences of their unsafe actions. If the company is going to be fair with them, then it must not merely *reprimand* them; but also, it must *reason with* them. "Come now, and let us reason together . . ." (Isaiah 1:18).
3. The "weapon" of *humiliation*. As used here, to humiliate a rebellious worker is to *lower his pride*. His pride is what makes him exalt himself against the will of his superiors . . . or the company. It should be firmly insisted that he do *what* he was instructed to do, and to do it the *way* he was instructed to do it. Failure to comply should lead to disciplinarian action.
4. The "weapon" of *submission*. When a worker has rebel thoughts . . . of committing unsafe acts . . . he should submit his self to the company. He should surrender his will to that of the company. The will of the company is that in the course of performing his work, he be productive, but more so that he be *safe*. If he fails to *submit to* the company, then he will *rebel against* the company. He will act in opposition to the company . . . and its safety program. To submit to the company is to *choose to not do* what he thought to do. To rebel against the company is to *choose to do* what he thought to do. Submission [to the company] is the key that unlocks his *obedience*. Resistance [against the company] is the key that unlocks his *disobedience*.

The "Ten Commandments" of Having a Safe Workplace

● Safety truth:

> *An honorable employee should not only be recognized for his years of **service** but also for his years of **safe work.***

A safe workplace is only made possible by safe workers.

Safe workers are those that obey [consistently] the "ten commandments" of having a safe workplace. Here they are:

1. DO NOT put any other goal before the Goal of Safety. Other goals can be the production goal, the quality goal, etc. Workers can get hurt while trying to be productive. They can get hurt while trying to ensure quality of what they produce.
2. DO NOT idolize anyone who is not a safe worker. Neither worship the ground that person walks on nor yield or surrender yourself to that person's will . . . what he or she wants you to do. What they want you to do may be unsafe, or may cause you to put yourself in jeopardy.
3. DO NOT dishonor the company's safety rules and regulations. Respect them . . . at all times. They're made with you in mind. They're established for your very safety.
4. DO NOT forget to rest. To rest is to cease from work. You have to be sensible to cease from work so you don't overwork yourself. In addition, you must give your physical body adequate rest. Make sure you get *enough* sleep. Sleep is rejuvenating power for your physical body. If your physical body isn't *rejuvenated,* then it won't be *ready* for the next work day. If it's not ready for the work ahead of it, it won't hold up to the demands that work may place upon it. It is then subject to collapse . . . or break down suddenly in physical strength and thereby become unable to continue doing the work. If your body can't go on, then you can't go on!
5. DO NOT despise the company for which you work. Despising the company you work for will lead to despising its safety rules and regulations. Despising its safety rules and regulations will lead [ultimately] to you shortening your days on earth.

6. DO NOT kill yourself. You can work yourself to death. Don't do too much while trying to do a job or finish it in time . . . whether before break time or quitting time. If you overexert yourself, you may hurt yourself.
7. DO NOT practice safety violation. In other words, don't make safety violation a habit. Don't get into the habit of committing the same safety violation over and over. Soon, you will develop the belief that you're getting away with it. Eventually, you'll begin to "get careless" with it. Unaware, an incident can come upon you like a thief in the night! Just as you cannot be prepared for a thief if you don't know when he's coming, you cannot be ready for an incident if you don't know when it is coming. Practicing safety violation is like playing Russian roulette. Russian roulette is a stunt in which one spins the cylinder of the revolver loaded with only one bullet, aims the muzzle at one's head, and pulls the trigger. You can "pull a stunt" so many times before it catches up with you. You can commit the same safety violation so many times before it becomes an incident with you.
8. DO NOT steal away to restricted areas or dangerous areas of the workplace. If you try to leave furtively and stealthily from where you're *supposed to be,* you may find yourself in a dangerous part of the workplace, where you can be *unexpectedly* hurt . . . or even killed. Someone who may work in that particular area, in the course of doing his work, may not know you're there and therefore may end up unknowingly hurting you or possibly killing you.
9. DO NOT lie to others about your incident. Tell them the truth about what actually happened to you . . . or with you. Lying about it can be leaving a hidden trap for a fellow worker . . . to fall in. Telling the truth about it will expose that hidden trap so that "the next man" doesn't fall into it. You should care about your coworker enough to inform . . . and warn . . . him or her about what happened to you, so that it doesn't happen to them.
10. DO NOT desire someone else's "possessions" in the workplace. What you desire you will *long for.* What you long for you will *lust after.* What you lust after you will *want strongly.* What you want

strongly you will try to get . . . by any means necessary. One's "possessions" in the workplace can include:

- Position (wanting strongly the job one holds)
- Prestige (wanting strongly the respect one has)
- Power (wanting strongly the authority one wields)
- Pride (wanting strongly the feeling of importance one experiences)
- Pay (wanting strongly the money one makes)
- Privileges (wanting strongly the special advantages one enjoys)
- Preferential treatment (wanting strongly the special treatment one receives)

When you want strongly what belongs to another, you may try to *sabotage* that person, to get it. However, your sabotage could cause that person's injury . . . or imminent death.

Sabotage is the deliberate destruction, disruption, or damage of equipment (or something else), as by *a dissatisfied employee*. A dissatisfied employee desires what another person in the workplace possesses and may seek to move that person out of his way . . . of getting what he wants strongly.

Getting Caught "Red-handed" . . . Or in a "Trap"

● Safety truth:

*Unsafe employees will try to teach you **short cuts**. Safe employees will try to be **shining examples** of workplace safety.*

The safety violations you *conceal* you will *continue to commit*.

If you continue to commit them, you will make it to the day when you won't be *fortunate*.

You will be *unfortunate*.

You will be unfortunate in one of two ways:

1. You will get caught in the act of committing your safety violation; or,
2. You will get hurt or killed.

The thief... if he continues stealing... will *eventually get caught.*
He will eventually get caught because he will *become complacent.*
When he does become complacent, he will *become careless.*
When he does become careless, he will *slip up.*
He will eventually make a mistake.

Don't be that thief!
Don't keep trying to "get away with" your safety violation.
Your safety violation is not worth it!

Caught "Red-handed": Receiving Punishment or Pardon

If you are caught *in the very act* of committing your safety violation and are brought before the company, you will receive either *punishment* or *pardon* from the company.

Receiving Punishment

If you are convicted of a safety violation, then the next immediate step is to be punished.

To be punished is to be subject to punishment.

The punishment assigned to a criminal who's convicted of a crime (or found guilty by the court) is called a sentence.

I call the punishment which a worker who's convicted of a safety violation may receive a "sentence."

Punishment can be one of two "sentences" you may receive:

1. A "death sentence." This is *termination.* You are fired for your safety violation. This punishment is for major safety violations. Major safety violations are "Cardinal Rules" violation.

2. A "prison sentence." This is *suspension*. You are given time off (without pay) for your safety violation. This punishment is for minor safety violations. Time off also serves the purpose of giving you time to think about what you did and be determined to make sure it doesn't ever happen again.

Receiving Pardon

Question: *Why would the company decide to release you from punishment for your safety violation?*
Certainly, *being forgiven* is better than *being fired!*

If you commit a safety violation and are *repentant* and want a second chance, the company does possess the power of pardon.
The company can *forgive* you of your safety violation.

✎ *Repentance is the key to forgiveness!*

Just as a convicted criminal who wants to be pardoned may throw his self on the mercy of the court, when you really feel remorse or self-reproach for the safety violation you've committed, you may also throw yourself at the mercy of the company. You can *ask* the company for mercy when you're being "sentenced for your crime."

The company has the power to punish and to pardon.
The company is not out to get anyone. It simply wants its workers to *be safe*.
To be safe is to *care*.
The company wants you to care about your own safety . . . and the safety of others.

The secret to pardon lies within the burden you must bear to convince the company of your genuine repentance and assure the company you won't commit that safety violation any more.
If you are convicted of a safety violation but the company doesn't punish you for it, then you may receive *pardon*. The company might tell you, "Go your way and commit that safety violation no more."

Caught in a "Trap": Your Resulting Condition

Even if you manage to avoid getting caught in the act of committing your safety violation, you yet take a chance on having *an incident*.

An incident is something that *actually happens*.

I call an incident that is the result of repeated safety violation *a trap*.

Steel mills recognize three types of incidents you can have in the workplace: (1) A near miss, (2) a doctor's case, and (3) a fatality.

There are three types of "traps" you can fall into as a result of your repeated safety violation. They are as follows:

1. A "squirrel trap." This type of trap is *harmless*. This is what I call a near miss. In a near miss, you can have:

    - A property damage
    - A preliminary
    - A first aid

In a "squirrel trap" (near miss), you experience a "close call."

2. A "bear trap." A bear trap will hurt a human being, if he gets caught in it! Similarly, this type of "trap" is *injurious or harmful*. In it you have *a doctor's case* for that first aid proves inadequate to handle the injury suffered. The injured person has to see a doctor. If the sustained injury is severe enough, it can result in *time off*. In a "bear trap," you get hurt.
3. A "death trap." This type of trap will claim your very life. In it you have *a fatality*. Losing your life is the ultimate price you pay for your repeated safety violation. In a "death trap," you die.

These three types of traps are ever present in the workplace.

You simply must do the right thing . . . in each and every instance.

Safety violation can cause you suffering . . . and the suffering can be severe . . . not only for you but also for your family and friends!

Keeping safe is one of the most positive ways of demonstrating your genuine care for yourself and your loved ones.

Don't get caught in a "trap!"

It's not necessarily guaranteed you'll come of it fortunately. You may get hurt or killed!

People getting hurt or killed is a *common event* in the workplace.

The workplace DEMANDS your daily respect!

"Trap" Type	Resulting Condition
A "Squirrel Trap"	You are *fortunate.*
A "Bear Trap"	You are *hurt.*
A "Death Trap"	You are *killed.*

Playing the Game of "Sudden Death"

● Safety truth:

*The feet of unsafe employees **run to** safety violation; but safe employees **remain** on the path of performing their work safely.*

A rebellious worker is a *hardheaded person.*

A hardheaded person is stubborn, continually *determined* to do what he wants to do . . . even if it's unsafe to do.

▶ A rebellious worker *practices* safety violation.
▶ A rebellious worker *plays with* his life.

In fact, a rebellious worker plays the game of "sudden death." Sudden death is death that happens suddenly . . . without warning. It comes upon you like a thief in the night.

Game Over: 4 Fatal Facts about the "Player"

1. **The "player" is reproved . . . often.** He is sharply reprimanded many times. He's warned time after time after time. He receives warning before destruction . . . many times.
2. **The "player" stubbornly adheres to his unsafe practices.** This is due to his pride. "Pride goeth before destruction . . ." (Proverbs 16:18). He's too proud to listen . . . no matter *how many* warnings he's mercifully given.
3. **The "player" will "lose the game."** If he keeps playing the game of "sudden death," he will lose the game. He will eventually be killed. It's just a matter of time.
4. **The "player" won't get another chance to "play."** When he dies, he won't be able to practice his safety violation any more. It will be "game over" for him. He will stop playing this game . . . whether by his *decision* or by his *death*.

W.H.E.E.L. of Fortune

● Safety truth:

> An **unseen** incident is as a net spread for an **unsuspecting** employee.

Steel mills have two types of workers: safe workers and unsafe workers.

Safe workers *respect* what can harm them.

Because they respect what can harm them, they keep themselves safe.

Because they keep themselves safe, they make the company glad.

Unsafe workers keep their unsafe practices.

Unsafe practices give them *pleasure*. Unsafe workers actually *enjoy* doing some things that are certainly unsafe.

The unsafe things they enjoy doing become their *work habits*.

Unsafe workers have unsafe habits!

I don't want you to take the risk of getting caught in the act of committing a safety violation. That would be unfortunate for you.

I don't want you to take the risk of getting hurt. That would be unfortunate for you.

I don't want you to take the risk of getting killed. That would be most unfortunate for you!

You should want to have *good fortune* in the workplace . . . not *bad fortune*.

There are *foolish habits* that can cause you to be an *unfortunate employee*.

There are *wise habits* that can cause you to be a *fortunate employee*.

Using the word WHEEL as an acronym, I let each letter stand for the following:

Wise
Habits (for)
Every
Employee (to)
Learn

Wise habits belong to *wise workers*.

Wise habits are the essential keys to having good fortune in the workplace.

Good fortune in the workplace is what a fortunate employee has.

8 *Wise Habits to Make You a Fortunate Employee*

1. **Learn the wise habit of REFUSING TO strive with fellow employees.** If you strive with fellow employees for wrongs they may have done towards you, then in all likelihood, you will want to take vengeance against them. If you take vengeance against them, you will get into trouble *along with* them. Moreover, vengeance can turn into violence. Violence in the workplace is a very serious concern . . . for the real possibility that someone could get seriously hurt or possibly killed. That would be unfortunate for you. Humble yourself to take the high path of peace. Handle the situation *the peaceful way.* Go to your

wrongdoers' superiors to get justice. That way, you'll be innocent of any wrongdoing towards them. The way of peace is an honorable way to being a fortunate employee.

2. **Learn the wise habit of REJOICING IN your fellow employees' good fortune.** This will indicate that your heart is *at peace* with them. When your heart is at peace with them, it will *enliven* you. It will make you *feel good*. It can bring healing to broken relationships you may have with them. It will make you want to forget about the past and fully enjoy them in the present . . . and the future.
   ▶ When you forgive, you *forget*.
   ▶ When you forgive, you *find healing*.

   You may find yourself wanting to celebrate with them. You may even wish to give them warmhearted gifts. You will just want the nightmare of being in conflict with them to be over. You will desire *reunion with them*. Reunion with them will really make you glad. You will be a fortunate employee . . . being fortunate to be reunited with them.

3. **Learn the wise habit of RELYING ON God to intervene into every situation you may encounter on the job.** The things you cannot *prevail over* in your own might or power, you need to *pray over*. What you pray over will be targeted for divine conquest. What you fail to pray over will defeat you. What defeats you on the job will cause you to have a series of unfortunate events on the job. You may have on-the-job training. Make sure you have on-the-job praying. It will come in handy in trying times on the job. Then you will be a fortunate employee.

4. **Learn the wise habit of REMAINING GRATEFUL for benefits you receive.** If you go through life being ungrateful for what others do for you, they will *feel unappreciated*. When they feel unappreciated, they may *lose the desire of heart* to help you. You really cannot afford to lose their "helping hand" . . . especially should you find yourself in a time of trouble. That would be unfortunate for you. " . . . but woe to him that is alone when he falleth; for he hath not another to HELP HIM UP," (Ecclesiastes 4:10).

5. **Learn the wise habit of RELEASING the spirit of love in you.** Don't suppress the spirit of love in you. Let the spirit of love be expressed in your attitude and actions. When you do not *allow*

the spirit of love to be seen in your actions, when you do wrong towards others, you suppress the spirit of love in you. Learn to allow the spirit of love to be revealed the way it should be . . . in you. *Where the spirit of love is absent, the spirit of hate will be present.* Your actions are *seeds*. Your actions of love are "seeds" of love that will produce for you "harvests" of love. On the contrary, your acts of hate are "seeds" of hate that will produce for you "harvests" of hate. (You reap what you sow.) The "harvests" of hate you reap in your own life, which are the results of "seeds" of hate you "sowed" towards others, will prove to be unfortunate for you.

6. **Learn the wise habit of RESPECTING financial/economic predictions of the company.** Don't despise what they say about the financial and economic future of the company. I'd worked eighteen years on my first job. When the day arrived that the owner gave a gloomy prediction of the company's financial and economic condition, I took warning! While the other workers *assumed* everything would be alright, I *acted*. I used my vacation time wisely . . . as I pursued and procured *another job* that was financially/economically stable. After five years of being established on my *new* job, the *old* one "went south." All the workers were laid off. That company was sold under new management. Barely half the workers were called back. Those that weren't called back had to find another job. Those that were called back were *uncertain* of how long that company would be in business. How unfortunate for them. Don't let that happen to you. That would be unfortunate for you.

7. **Learn the wise habit of RETAINING what is beneficial to you and RELINQUISHING what is not beneficial to you.** If something doesn't benefit you, then it's no good to you. What is no good to you should be considered *trash*. Trash is what you throw away or get rid of. What is good to you should be considered *treasure*. Treasure is what you keep or hold on to. It can be unfortunate for you to get rid of something that could benefit you. You might miss it . . . once it's gone. It can be unfortunate for you to keep something that doesn't benefit you . . . especially in a time when you *really need* it to serve you, and serve you well.

8. **Learn the wise habit of REFRAINING FROM every kind of wrong . . . in the workplace.** Every kind of wrong can be *harmful to you . . . in some way.* Every kind of wrong you may commit can work out to your evil, and not your good. The wrong you commit is the "seed" for the "harvest" of some evil experience you will "reap" or have. An evil experience as a consequence of your wrong will be unfortunate for you.

Holding the Person in Charge Responsible

● Safety truth:

> *An employee who's a voracious time saver will try to **gain time** by choosing to **give up** his safe practices.*

A steel mill must be *managed.*
Managed, it is managed by *managers.*
The highest ranking manager of a steel mill is called *the general manager.*
The general manager is the head of a steel mill. That particular person is, indeed, the person in charge. (But with great power comes great responsibility.)
He . . . or she . . . is in charge of *that steel mill's whole operation.*
That steel mill's whole operation is made up of separate operations.
One of these separate operations is that steel mill's most important operation. It is that steel mill's *safety operation.*

Just Cause

The general manager has the Herculean task of making *the workplace* of the steel mill he heads, *secure.*
The general manager must be *a firm leader* of the workplace.
As a firm leader of the workplace, he has to have *full control* over his subordinates.
He has to have *full authority* over those that work under him.

A *secure* workplace [one kept tight] has the most favorable condition to be a *safe* workplace. Otherwise, a *loose* workplace will be led by the general manager. He will be over a workplace where workers, who lack a sense of restraint or responsibility, will *run loose*.

☞ *When workers run loose, incidents run up!*

Justice Administration

The general manager makes the workplace secure by *justice*.
Justice to which I refer is the administering of deserved punishment.
The general manager makes the workplace secure (keeps it from becoming loose) by administering *deserved punishment* to safety violators.
Safety violators who're deservingly punished will serve as powerful examples to the rest of the workers who might think about "pulling the same stunt."
In this moral sense, justice will *strike fear* in the hearts of the workers.
The workers must learn to fear what can harm them.
They must learn not to make light of what can hurt or kill them.

☞ *Safety is no joke!*

"Justice of the Peace"

The general manager is "justice of the peace" of his workplace. He has authority to *act upon* safety violations committed in his workplace.
Notwithstanding, the general manager must be a *person of integrity*.
▶ A person of integrity **does what's right.**
▶ A person of integrity **doesn't take bribes.**
If the general manager takes "bribes" from safety violators who're convicted of their safety violations, he will *let them go*.
Letting them go will lead to a loose workplace. Other safety violators will also *expect* to be "let go." They can charge the general manager with *partiality*.

Partiality can get the general manager in trouble. Just as a justice of the peace can be removed from office for corrupt or unlawful conduct, the general manager can be *removed from office* for corrupt or unlawful conduct.

Partiality is corrupt or unlawful conduct.

↯ *A person of integrity has no respect of persons!*

Judgment Flood: "The Dam Keeper"

When the general manager allows the workplace (he's over) to become loose, he practically *overthrows* the workplace. He brings about the downfall of that workplace.

A *loose workplace* will experience a *large increase* in incidents.

A flood of judgment is coming.

A flood of incidents is on the way.

▶ A flood of water can **destroy an inhabited place.**
▶ A flood of incidents can **destroy a workplace.**

The workplace that has an abundant flow of incidents will, in all probability, be *closed down.* Its operations will be either temporarily or permanently stopped.

When incidents (property damages, personal injuries, and perhaps fatalities) *pile up,* that workplace's incident rate will *go up.*

If the incident rate is sure to *go up,* then company profits are sure to *go down.*

When the company starts losing more money than what it's actually making with one of its divisions, it's good as "going in the hole."

A division of a company is like a branch on a plant. If the plant isn't able to bear fruit through one of its branches, the gardener will prune that particular branch.

Likewise, if the company isn't able to produce profits through one of its divisions, then its executive officers will have to consider the real possibility of having to "prune the plant" of that particular division that's costing them more money than it's making for them. That division in question may get "cut off" from among the other remaining divisions of the company.

This is why it is so very important the general manager (who's over a division of the company) be what I call a "dam keeper."

A dam keeper is one who keeps or preserves a dam.

A dam is designed to hold back a flood of water.

Similarly, the general manager must keep or preserve the "dam" that holds back a "flood" of incidents . . . in the workplace.

This "dam" to which I refer, which restrains a "flood" of incidents in the workplace, is the general manager's *zero tolerance for MANY incidents*.

- ▶ He may tolerate *few* incidents.
- ▶ He should not tolerate *many* incidents.

Many incidents are an *evil omen* of horrible consequences . . . such as a fatality.

A fatality is "the big one" that every workplace wants to surely avoid.

If many incidents begin to happen, then it's time for the general manager to:

1. *Put his foot down,* letting the workers know that he most certainly will not have that. This will help the workers to refocus on being safe. For those who "don't get the message" and leave the safety meeting to commit safety violations *anyway,* the general manager must show them he's serious . . . about the safety of the workplace. He must deal with them accordingly. He must make examples out of them . . . for the others' sake and the sake of a safe workplace.
2. *Put into action* some kind of recovery plan, to get the workplace back on track . . . of being safe. He will have to "round up" his "cabinet," which may consist of the assistant general manager, safety director, assistant safety director, superintendents, general foremen, and other key position holders.

The general manager must preserve his *zero tolerance for many incidents*. If he loses it, then he stands to lose his workplace . . . and his work position.

- He cannot afford to *excuse* safety violations . . . often.
- He cannot afford to *expect* the workers to keep safe without his ongoing encouragement and moral support.

- He cannot afford to *exclude* the real possibility of people losing their genuine respect for what can hurt or kill them.

The general manager must do his best to make sure the very people who work under him are "wearing" an H.A.R.D. hat, not a hard head! He has to be continually concerned about them having extreme respect for what has real potential to harm them.

He is the person the company *has in charge.*

He is the person the company *holds responsible . . . for what happens in the workplace he heads.*

SAFETY COUNSEL FOR YOU TO CONSIDER

- Where there is no *respect* for what has dangerous potential, there will be *regret*.
- Machines can be your *best friends* . . . and your *worst enemies*.
- Looks can be deceiving. Because it may look safe doesn't mean it is safe. So *confirm* it's safe before you *continue*.
- Just when you think you've seen *it all*, you may see *something new*.
- *Harmony* doesn't necessarily mean that *harm* isn't present. Enjoy your workday . . . and expect the unexpected.
- Don't depend on *complex instruction* so much as *common sense*.
- If it *looks* unsafe, *leave it alone!* It's better safe than sorry.
- The workplace is a place of *employment* . . . not *entertainment*.
- Let the *horses* play. Let the *hired hands* play it safe!
- What you *fail* to investigate may be a hidden trap you may *fall into*.
- Know the vital difference between *assumption* and *assurance*.
- You *encourage* other workers to be safe when they see you *exemplify* how to be safe . . . or do something the safe way.

2

Wearing E.Y.E. Protection: Value Your Vision!

● Safety truth:

> *The true purpose of the company's reproof is to turn an employee from his **wrong way** of doing his job to the **right way** of doing it.*

> *Where there is no vision, the people perish . . .*

> —PROVERBS 29:18

You have *vision*.
However, I'm not talking about your physical eyesight or your *ability to see*.
What I'm referring to is your *ability to understand*.
You must not only *know what can harm you*.
You must also *understand how it can harm you*.

Using the word *EYE* as an acronym, I let each letter stand for the following:

Enlightenment (for)
Your
Enrichment

Understanding how dangerous things can harm you is enlightenment for your enrichment.

Enlightenment for your enrichment is *empowerment.*

If the company hopes to see its employees *impress* it, then the company must *empower* them with good understanding . . . of how:

- Operating equipment works
- Ongoing plant work must be continually respected
- Overbearing or overconfident employees can get hurt . . . or killed.

Where there is little or no *understanding* of what can harm you, there is *undermining* of a critical sense of safety.

↳ *What you don't understand can overcome you!*

Seeing through S.A.F.E.T.Y. Glasses

- Safety truth:

    *Misunderstanding someone can lead to **making a mistake** . . . which might harm him or you.*

S.A.F.E.T.Y. Glasses help you to "see" how to do your job the right way and the safest way.

Using the word *SAFETY* as an acronym, I let each letter stand for the following:

Systematic
Approach
Fundamentals (of)
Effective
Training (for)
You

There are systematic approach fundamentals of effective training the company should know and implement in its on-the-job training.

7 Systematic Approach Fundamentals of Effective Training

1. **Ensure the employee being trained "passes" the initial tests before "graduating" him to successive lessons.** In each training session, make sure he gets *good understanding*. Good understanding is the key to proper preparation. Proper preparation produces a properly trained worker. A properly trained worker is equipped to be a practically safe worker.
2. **Don't rush the employee to learn.** Everyone isn't a "quick learner." His quick training may fail to have instilled in him some essential quality or essential understanding, the lack of which may ultimately prove to be the cause of his unfortunate injury . . . or his unexpected death.
3. **Give the employee sufficient information and instruction.** Don't shortchange him on any of these very important areas. A poorly equipped army will to be an ineffective army. So a poorly trained employee will prove to be an ineffective employee . . . and very possibly an unsafe employee.
4. **Welcome all his observations, questions, and concerns which he may have.** Leave no stone of uncertainty unturned. Assure the employee. Put all his fears to rest. *Training should begin with trust.*
5. **Forcefully express . . . and make abundantly clear . . . the company's complete intolerance of safety violation.** For the sake of that person's life (and the lives of others), don't sugarcoat anything. Make it plain and simple. Let him know the utter seriousness of this matter. *A serious trainer must be a serious speaker.*
6. **Though his *work ethic* may be closely watched, pay very close attention to his *work attitude*.** It will determine if he is malleable or mainly concerned about doing things *his own way*. He must be willing to do things the company's prescribed way, in accordance with its safe-training practices. Not his will but the company's will be done, in safe performance of the work.
7. **Determine his strengths and weaknesses.** This will help to place him where he will serve best and be safest at doing his work. To place him in a work area he's *weak in* is to place him in potential

jeopardy. The work he's weak in he won't be confident in. Find out what he's *strong in* and train him in that field of work. What he's strong in will ultimately produce strong confidence in him to do . . . and to do most effectively . . . and most safely.

Value Your Vision!

Value your vision.
Your vision is your *ability to see.*
To see is to *understand.*
If you don't understand what you're doing while you're doing it, then you're *working blind.*
Working blind is sure to lead to your injury . . . even potentially your death. So make sure you UNDERSTAND your job: how to do it correctly and in the safest possible manner.

> *Ignorance can lead to incidents!*

Ignorance means you don't know or understand.
Don't be an *ignorant* worker.
Be an *informed* worker.
The company must search and stamp out all ignorance it may find in the workplace.
It has a moral obligation to provide its employees with the necessary information/instruction which they didn't previously possess.

> *If you don't know or understand something, don't act like you do know!*

You thereby deceive the company that it has done its job of making sure you're properly trained. You're then nothing more than an incident just waiting to happen! It's just a matter of time!

> *Your ignorance jeopardizes your individual safety!*

You should **be afraid** to do . . . or even attempt to do . . . any job which you don't have good understanding of, especially without the presence and precious experience of a veteran worker. Never try to "play hero," to "save the day" when the production goal is in jeopardy, for whatever reason. Leave that to the veterans!

Seeing a Company of Horses

● Safety truth:

> *If the company fails to **instruct** its employees in the way of safety, incidents will have ample opportunity to **increase.***

I refer to a steel mill company as a "company of horses." The company is comprised basically of divisions I call "horses."

I call them "horses" because they "run with the vision" of the company.

The vision of the company should dominantly deal with the company *seeing* itself as a safe workplace.

> *Where there is no vision, the people perish . . .*
>
> —PROVERBS 29:18

If the company *cannot see* itself as a safe workplace, then the people's *sense of safety* will *disappear gradually.*

▶ When the people's sense of safety *disappears,* the company's hope of having a safe workplace *dies.*

▶ When the people's sense of safety *disappears,* the "horses" of the company are *doomed* to become "crippled" or unable to "run with the vision" of the company, where safety is the main concern.

A crippled horse is useless.

A crippled horse is usually killed.

Similarly, a crippled "horse" of the company is "useless."

A crippled "horse" or division of the company might be "killed." In other words, its very operations might be shut down *permanently.*

Workplace safety is the key to preventing a "lame horse."

If the people who work at a division of the company work safe . . . and keep safe . . . then the "horse" they "ride on" will be kept safe . . . from becoming "crippled."

♘ *The safety of the "horse" depends on the safety of its "riders!"*

A Heads-up for the "Horse Riders": 3 Protection Principles

The "horse riders" to whom I refer are the very people who work at a division of the company.

As a "horse rider" or worker at a division of the company, here are three things that you can do to protect the "horse" you "ride on" or the company division you work at:

Protection Principle #1: DEPEND ON the safety rules and regulations to keep you safe. Don't try to *figure out* something you don't know anything about or don't understand; rather, *find* a veteran worker, who knows how to do something [safely], and knows how it operates . . . or is supposed to work. This will help keep you safe and thereby will help protect the division you work at, by means of keeping safe in the course of doing your job.

Protection Principle #2: DEFER TO those safety rules and regulations so they'll lead you safely in the course of your work. When you don't know whether or not something is safe or don't know what to do in a situation where your safety may be at stake, recall the safety rules and safety regulations! Think about them. You have to remember they are designed *with you in mind*. They are *for you . . . and your personal protection*. This will help keep you safe and thereby help protect the division you work at, by means of keeping safe in the course of doing your job.

Protection Principle #3: DO NOT try to "outsmart" personal injury or personal death. Respect [continually] what has the potential to harm you. Don't "flirt with death." Don't take dangerous risks! Resist every temptation to "put on a show" in the workplace, to be "impressive" to other workers . . . who may witness your injury . . . or even your death.

This will help keep you safe and thereby help protect the division you work at, by means of keeping safe in the course of doing your job.

Seeing the Company as a "Correctional Facility" . . . Without the "Prison Mentality"

● Safety truth:

> *Where there is no **concern** for safety there will be no **conquest** of incidents.*

The workplace is not a *prison*, but a *production facility*. Notwithstanding, people who work in the workplace sometimes exhibit *unsafe conduct*.

Unsafe conduct has to be *corrected* by the company.

The company is seen as a "correctional facility" . . . without the "prison mentality."

It seeks to correct unsafe conduct of its employees.

4 Things You Should Not Do . . . When the Company Corrects You

1. **You should not *despise* the company's thought of your own safety.** Your own safety is the company's highest concern. Whether or not you believe it, the company has your best interest at heart. Correction is provoked by the company's thought of your own safety.
2. **You should not *feel* the company "picks on" you.** The company doesn't bully its employees. It doesn't treat them in an overbearing or intimidating manner. The company knows . . . and respects the fact . . . that it can get into trouble for picking on people. The company doesn't seek to *pick on* you. Instead, it seeks to *protect* you.
3. **You should not *think* the company "gets a kick out of" correcting you.** Probably contrary to your belief, the company doesn't enjoy punishing anyone. Whenever the company metes

out *punishment,* it's for the *personal improvement* of the employee. Simply put, the company wants you . . . its employee . . . to "do better," especially where safety is concerned.
4. **You should not *resist* the company's "parental influence" over you.** Just as it's within a father's rights to correct his child, it's within the company's rights to correct its employees. But, the company has to be very careful to not *abuse* you. Not only can company abuse lead to a *loss* of an employee, it can also lead to a *lawsuit*.

9 Golden Nuggets of Knowledge about the Company and Its Continuing Safety Quest

1. **The company encounters SITUATIONS for which it has no SOLUTIONS.** When it has a situation but has no solution for it, it has to *seek a solution*. A solution exists . . . for that every situation has a solution; but sometimes, the solution has to be *sought out*. An *unknown solution* must be *uncovered* . . . or *revealed*. In its safety quest, the company must pursue a practical solution to a safety problem. It may seek a solution among its *own employees* or *other companies*.
2. **The company is UNPREPARED FOR something when it is UNAWARE OF something.** The company is unprepared for the defeat of its safety purpose for its workplace when it is not aware of unsafe employees in its workplace. The company has to learn who its *problem employees* are. Its problem employees will continually prevent it from reaching its safety goal. The company must *discover* who they are and *deal with* them accordingly . . . if its safety quest is to be successful.
3. **The company whose employees BELIEVE they cannot be safe will not BE safe.** If they don't *believe* they can be safe, then the company won't *achieve* its safety goal. In sports, the coach has to depend on his players to win the game . . . with his guidance. Similarly, the company has to *depend on* its employees to reach . . . and retain . . . the safety goal . . . with the company's guidance. The company must *find a way* to inspire faith in its employees, to cause them to believe in themselves, that they can be safe . . . and be the safest workplace in its industry.

4. **The company HAS "wounded workers" that need to be HEALED.** Workers can be wounded:
   ▶ Physically (working with an injured body part)
   ▶ Mentally (working with psychological abuse)
   ▶ Emotionally (working with hurt souls and hearts)
   ▶ Relationally (working with broken relationships)
   ▶ Financially (working with financial debt)
   Wounded workers are walking incidents waiting to happen. They need to *be healed* before they *become hurt* . . . in the workplace. The company runs a high risk when it allows these *individuals* to work, who might end up having *incidents*. The company doesn't know what's all going on in the "world" of their hearts and minds. There could be "world war" going on within them, while they work *quietly;* then suddenly, a *quick incident*.
5. **The company does not work MIRACLES; however, it does work MEN.** The company has to be very careful how it works its workers. It must be careful to not overwork them. As a real warning, *overworked workers* will have *opportunities* to have incidents. The company cannot "do the impossible" by keeping its workers safe . . . as it overworks them. Then is the company "asking for it."
6. **The company cannot FORESEE dangers, but it can FORECAST dangerous conditions.** For example, the company cannot foresee a tornado; but, it can forecast dangerous weather conditions (via the National Weather Service), which may usher in a tornado. By forecasting dangerous conditions, the company gives its employees time to act or to take cover. Such time can prove critical, which could save someone from a *lasting injury;* or, it could save someone's *life*.
7. **The company does not DETECT every potential danger, but it does DISCOVER some.** The company must maintain a *seek-and-destroy mentality* regarding potentially dangerous areas and dangerous conditions of the workplace, which have not been noticed or never addressed. It must continually seek what is unsafe. Then when it does *find* something unsafe, it must immediately act to *fix* it. Concerning its ever striving to have a safe workplace, the company isn't *perfect,* but it is *purposed* to reach its safety goal. Hats off to the company for its noble attempts to attain to a safe workplace . . . for all of its employees.

8. **The company is a MASS PRODUCER . . . and must be a MASTER COMMUNICATOR.** A lot of *production* goes on in the workplace. A lot of *communication* should also go on in the workplace. A lot of people may work for the company. A lot of people make a large audience the company will have to engage. Where there is no *communication to the workers,* there will be no *commitment to working safe.* The company is mainly responsible for keeping morale up . . . in the workplace. Its workers have to *hear from* it . . . frequently. Wherefore, frequent safety meetings are ideal. Notwithstanding, the employees *need* to see the company's face and hear the company's voice . . . often. This is a powerful key to keeping up morale among the workers.
9. **The company is able to INTERACT with other companies, and should be able to INTERPRET other companies' actions.** Companies in the same line of work *compete;* but, they can *come together* and learn from one another. If one company is *failing* in a specific area, it can *see how* another company is *succeeding* in that same area. But the one company must interpret the actions/operations of the other company. A safe company should be apt to "teach" other companies struggling with safety issues, its safety principles and safety practices. It's just the moral thing to do. It's the right thing to do. It's the honorable thing to do. What company takes pleasure in the injuries and fatalities of other companies?

Seeing Dollar Signs: The "Wrong Way" to Wealth

● Safety truth:

> *Where safety laws are **obeyed**, the safety goal will be **obtained**.*

Some workers in the workplace are *money-driven.*
Money-driven workers want all the overtime they can get.
Actually, they spend *too much time* in the workplace . . . when it's not *mandatory* but *voluntary.*
▶ They want to **make** *a lot of money.*
▶ They want to **have** *a lot of money.*

So they set out in the workplace to "work their butts off," to make all the money they possibly can.

What would I say to these money-driven people in the workplace?

> *Labour not to be rich: cease from thine own wisdom.*
>
> —PROVERBS 23:4

When you *work* to "be rich" or have a lot of money, you *wear yourself out!*
Wearing yourself out can harm your physical body.
Your physical body is the *only one* you have. Take very good care of it! Appreciate it. Cherish it. Do every thing in your power to preserve it.
Recognize that when you overwork your physical body, you do it a great injustice. You show lack of genuine concern for it. You see your physical body only as being to you *a tool.*
A tool is used to build things.
It is unwise . . . and unsafe . . . to try to *build wealth with your body.*

This is the *wisdom of the money-driven worker.*
The wisdom of the money-driven worker is *foolish.*
Because his wisdom is foolish, he should cease from it.
Because he should cease from it, it is *not good.*
What is not good is *evil.*
What is evil is *harmful.*
His foolish wisdom can cause him to harm himself!

✥ *Overworking can be an evil omen!*

Obtaining wealth requires *wise planning.*
Wise planning "charts your course," to reach the "destination" of wealth.
The "destination" of wealth is then your financial goal.
Your financial goal requires *a financial plan of action.* "Without counsel [a plan of action] purposes are disappointed," (Proverbs 15:22). Without a *plan of action* your *purpose to obtain wealth* will be disappointed.

✥ *To obtain financial wealth, you need a financial plan!*

To work without a financial plan is to *work blind*.

To work blind is to work *not seeing how* you can possibly obtain wealth.

To work blind is to work feverishly, working all the overtime hours you can . . . that your physical body will let you.

Actually, in this manner, you're not *working towards wealth*. Instead, you're *working yourself to death!*

Upsetting the Balance of Your Life

Overtime causes you to spend too much time in the workplace.
Too much time in the workplace will upset the balance of your life.
It will eat away at your time to:

- Be with your family
- Take care of business (after work)
- Enjoy your favorite pastime
- Exercise
- Rest

There's life after work!
Work (in overtime) produces an unbalanced life.
An unbalanced life is an unhealthy life.

An unhealthy life won't produce *good success* no more than an unhealthy tree won't produce *good fruit*.

Good fruit or favorable results should be what the "tree" of your life produces.

Seeing an Unsafe Thought as a "Seducer" and a "Slayer"

- Safety truth:

> *The company doesn't have the **right** to expect its employees to be safe if it doesn't supply them with the **resources** with which to be safe.*

An unsafe thought is a thought to do something unsafe.

Every worker, at some time or another, has an unsafe thought.

As surely as they will have the *thought* to do something unsafe, they will have the *temptation* to do something unsafe.

To *resist* the temptation to do something unsafe, they have to *rethink* what they thought to do that was unsafe.

Workers must not only be *thinkers.*

They must also be *rethinkers.*

Rethinkers reconsider their actions before executing them.

An unsafe thought can *seduce* you.

If you think about doing something that is unsafe *long enough,* you may let your heart turn aside to unsafe ways.

Don't go astray in the path of unsafe thinking!

An unsafe thought is a seed for an unsafe act.

An unsafe act is a dangerous risk.

A dangerous risk one takes *exposes* him to real danger.

A safe worker doesn't allow himself to be seduced by an unsafe thought.

An unsafe thought can *slay* you.

An unsafe thought has thrown down many wounded in the workplace. Many workers have been "slain" or harmed by an unsafe thought.

▶ An unsafe thought is not your *friend.*
▶ An unsafe thought is your *enemy.*

Your mind is a thinking machine.

As a thinking machine, your mind [you] must *think safety.*

Thinking safety is the starting point to working safely.

An unsafe thought can *seduce* you and *slay* you.

An unsafe thought is not good for you.

An unsafe thought is harmful to you.

You simply must discipline yourself to bring every unsafe thought to the obedience of safety rules and regulations.

Rethink it!

Consider the cost before carrying it out.

Ask yourself the question: *Can I really afford to do this?*

Seeing the Great Wall of C.H.I.N.A.

● Safety truth:

> *The key of knowledge is to unlock your **safety** . . . not your **superego**.*

As far as safety goes, the workplace can be *surrounded by* a great wall of protection.
A great wall of protection is *situated within* the workplace itself.
The workplace itself has to have safe workers.
Safe workers have *safe habits*.
Safe habits induce no accidents.

Using the word *CHINA* as an acronym, I let each letter stand for the following:

Common
Habits (that)
Induce
No
Accidents

You see, it is the safe habits that are *common* among safe workers which form this great wall of protection . . . around the workplace.

☞ *Safe habits are the key to a safe workplace!*

Where there are no *safe habits* there will be *sorrowful consequences*.
If the company can succeed at filling the workplace with safe workers, it can "build" a great wall of protection around the workplace.

The Significant Difference between a "Good" Worker and a "Safe" Worker

Of course, the company wishes to have good workers working for it. Nevertheless, the company has to realize two very significant things where safety is concerned:

1. A good worker (one who's consistent at being productive) isn't necessarily a *safe worker.*
2. A safe worker (one who's consistent at being safe) isn't necessarily a *good worker.*

Whereas a good worker will get much done, a safe worker may only get little done. A safe worker's highest concern is for *safety* . . . not *production.*

What the company needs . . . and should most definitely strive to obtain . . . are workers who're both productive and safe.

What good is good production with human injuries?

What good is safe performance with poor production?

Thus, a sense of balance must be brought to bear.

Having good production and safe performance **gladdens** *the company.*

Having good production and human injuries **grieves** *the company.*

There is no real profit when the production goal is attained but the safety goal isn't.

This is why it is so very important that workers' *work habits* not only be closely watched but also their *safe habits . . . or unsafe habits . . .* be carefully observed.

▶ Safe habits should be ***commended.***
▶ Unsafe habits should be ***condemned.***

Workers, who consistently work safe, have *purity* of work, which will make them ***secure.***

Workers, who consistently work unsafe, have *perversion* of work, which will make them ***subject to exposure.*** This simply means what they do "in the dark" or unbeknownst to others will come "to the light" or for everyone to see or know.

Purity of work (that is, work free of unsafe habits) will lead to that worker's joy.

Perversion of work (that is, work free of safe habits) will lead to that worker's sorrow.

Do You Have a Dangerous Sport?

The worker who has an unsafe practice has a *dangerous sport*. He likes . . . or may even love . . . his unsafe practice for the fact that it may give him some degree of pleasure.

If you have an unsafe practice, then you have a dangerous sport.
▶ A dangerous sport can result in your ***debilitating injury.***
▶ A dangerous sport can result in your ***death.***
You need a *safe sport*.
You need to learn to like . . . or even love . . . safe practices.
Safe practices are the beginning stages of safe habits.
Safe habits are the key to a safe work shift.
A safe work shift means a safe workday.
A safe workday is a single step to a safe workweek.
A safe workweek is the pattern for a safe month.
A safe month is the extended pattern for a safe year.
A safe year begins with a safe sport.

Seeing a "Super Typhoon" of Incidents

● Safety truth:

> In the workplace are found **men, machines,** and **methods.** Unfortunately, also found there are **misinterpretation, mistakes,** and **mishaps.**

When the workplace is enjoying a time of peace and prosperity, it isn't necessarily safe from a "typhoon" of incidents.

A "typhoon" of incidents can come out of nowhere . . . without warning. It can catch the company (and the workers) completely off guard.

The company cannot prepare for what it cannot foresee. All it can do is keep an eye out for a "typhoon" of incidents.

A "typhoon" of incidents can destroy a workplace.

A workplace which suffers far too many incidents is "doomed" to be closed or have its whole operation shut down.

▶ Safe workers ***get clear of*** a "typhoon" of incidents.
▶ Unsafe workers ***get caught in*** a "typhoon" of incidents.

No workplace in the world can withstand the destructive force of a "super typhoon" of incidents.

Wherefore, the company must take serious warning of a rash of incidents. If the workplace has an outbreak of many incidents within a brief period, it should most definitely serve as a warning sign.

A *rash of incidents* can "grow" or become a *rushing, mighty "windstorm" of incidents.* Once this happens, widespread destruction in the workplace is inevitable.

A "super typhoon" of incidents can lead to:

● *Destruction* (of company property)
● *Debilitation* (of job injury)
● *Death* (of an employee)

Simply put, the workers will be either *safe* or *sorry* . . . *for not being safe.* They really cannot afford to take Safety lightly.

Being safe should be one of their lifetime commitments.

M.I.A.M.I. Heat

Sometimes, a workplace can "feel" or experience what I call M.I.A.M.I. heat.

Using the word *MIAMI* as an acronym, I let each letter stand for the following:

Missing
In
Action (for)
Major
Incidents

Workers having *minor* incidents usually get by without a scratch . . . or, with only minor bruises. They can continue to work. They don't have to "go missing" in the workplace. They don't require time off . . . for any recuperation.

But workers having *major* incidents usually get hurt . . . or sometimes killed.

Those that *get hurt* end up "missing in action" *temporarily . . . or possibly permanently, if the injury they sustained is a debilitating one.* They have to be "off work" for a recuperative period of time.

However, those that *get killed* end up "missing in action" *permanently.* Their "time off" is permanent. They don't come back.

▶ Dead employees don't **return** to the workplace.
▶ Dead employees **retire** to the burial place . . . or the graveyard.

Every workplace must beware of M.I.A.M.I. heat.

It can be *destructive to its enterprise.*

It can be *deadly to its employees.*

If a substantial number of employees aren't *available* to work, then the overall production goal of the company won't be *attainable.*

Quality has its value.

Quantity also has its value.

Understandably then, though quality takes *precedence* over quantity, quantity still is a *principal requirement.*

The company wants:

- Safe work shifts
- Quality products/services
- Good production

These collectively comprise the "1-2-3 punch" which workers must deliver, for the company [they work for] to conquer success.

In the Event of Your D.E.A.T.H.

Housekeeping is key to having a safe workplace.
Terrific housekeeping *minimizes* incidents.
Terrible housekeeping *maximizes* incidents.
Terrible housekeeping can cause your D.E.A.T.H.

Using the word *DEATH* as an acronym, I let each letter stand for the following:

Dangerous
Experience
Arising (from
Terrible
Housekeeping

In the event of your dangerous experience arising from terrible housekeeping, you should report it.
A reported incident should be investigated.
An investigated incident should yield beneficial findings.
Beneficial findings pave the way for continual improvement of workplace conditions.
Workplace conditions play a crucial role in workplace safety.

14 Glorious Facts about Good Housekeeping

1. **Good housekeeping *eliminates* all kinds of hazards.** This includes trip hazards.
2. **Good housekeeping *exposes* hidden traps or unseen dangerous conditions.** It's just one more wonderful way of looking out for yourself . . . and your fellow workers.
3. **Good housekeeping *earns* for the workplace a good name.** Visitors will observe the *operation* and the *condition* of your workplace. What they *remember* seeing they may very well *report*.
4. **Good housekeeping *excites* employees with a real sense of pride.** You should take pride in your workplace. Have enough pride in it to keep it looking good!
5. **Good housekeeping *equips* employees with a powerful safety tool.** You don't have to be a maid to clean up your work area! A workplace is as a house. A house has rooms. A workplace has work areas. As a clean person will keep his/her room clean, a clean worker will keep his/her work area clean.
6. **Good housekeeping *ensures* a safe place to work.** Where there is no *housekeeping* there will be *harmful conditions*. You must simply get this into your head and get it cleaned up!
7. **Good housekeeping *expresses* the best means for bringing about a clean workplace.** A clean workplace is an impressive workplace. An impressive workplace can be a powerful eye-catcher for prospective customers.
8. **Good housekeeping *exemplifies* a good habit.** A good habit should never be broken. A good habit should be learned by others . . . and respected by all.
9. **Good housekeeping *examines* what might otherwise be overlooked.** No stone is left unturned. Cleaning can not only be removal of filth but also removal of obstructions which can cause unsafe conditions.
10. **Good housekeeping *excludes* a careless attitude.** Cleanliness is a sure sign you care! It is a sure sign that you care not only about your own safety but also the safety of others.
11. **Good housekeeping *exists* in a successful workplace.** A successful workplace is a safe workplace. A safe workplace

practices good housekeeping. Where there is no *housekeeping* there will be a *hefty price* which workers will pay.

12. **Good housekeeping *establishes* a moral sense of duty.** It should make you duty-bound to do it! You shouldn't have to be made to do it. You should want to do it simply because it's a mighty pillar of a safe workplace.
13. **Good housekeeping *effects* a positive change of atmosphere.** I don't know of a single worker who enjoys working in a torn-down workplace, where practically everything is out of order, or out of line. Where there is no *organization* there will be *obstruction*.
14. **Good housekeeping *evolves* as workplace conditions may change.** Where good housekeeping *ends,* that workplace *experiences* incident growth. Incidents can only be lowered in a clean environment.

Seeing the Wisdom of My Words

● Safety truth:

*If a safety talk is **boring** to you, it may not be **beneficial** to you. You have to **respect** it, to **reap** its preservation power.*

I want you to see the wisdom of my words.

The wisdom of my words conveys an ultimate message for every employee on earth.

That ultimate message is:

🌎 *TO AVOID SAFETY VIOLATION, LET EVERY EMPLOYEE HAVE HIS OR HER OWN INSTRUCTION OF WISDOM.* 🌎

Wisdom is a wonderful combination of knowledge and understanding.
▶ Knowledge is *information* you have.
▶ Understanding is *insight* you have.
Wisdom demands you have both.
Wisdom *instructs* you in having great respect for what can harm you.

Safe workers are only safe continually if they're *wise workers*.

Wise workers are those that have been instructed in wisdom . . . of workplace safety.

Wise workers avoid safety violation.

They avoid safety violation because:

1. They *genuinely fear* getting hurt or killed.
2. They are *self-disciplined* to do things the safe way.
3. They see safety as no *accident* but rather as an *attainable goal*.

I firmly believe that until you *choose* to be a wise worker, you won't be a safe worker consistently. In all likelihood, you will choose to be safe *when* others . . . especially important figures . . . are around. But will you choose to be safe *when* others are not around?

You see, wise workers are safe whether or not anyone is around.

People can *pretend* to be safe workers. As a matter of fact, when they find themselves alone, their mask of pretense comes off and their *hidden* unsafe practices are *brought out of hiding*.

❦ *To pretend to be safe is to put your self in jeopardy!*

Seeing Your Safety through the Eyes of Your Loved Ones: Ten Golden Facts

● Safety truth:

> *Employees may have **good jobs**, but they also need **good judgment**.*

1. Your loved ones that love you will suffer long with you because they're *determined* that you do away with your unsafe habits. Your unsafe habits cause them concern.
2. Your loved ones that love you may be kind about your unsafe conduct, not wanting to offend you. But your stubbornness can anger them and cause them to "go off" on you . . . in a very highly emotional outburst.

3. Your loved ones that love you don't envy you for your unsafe habits. They know that a single unsafe habit can easily be the key to unlock the unexpected event of your very death.
4. Your loved ones that love you don't boast about your unsafe conduct. Your unsafe conduct causes them concern. They don't see *glory* in what you unsafely do. They see only *grief* in what you unsafely do.
5. Your loved ones that love you are not too proud to "tell you about yourself." Though they may seek every opportunity to honor you while trying to "get through" to you, they're not beyond taking it to the next level: open rebuke.
6. Your loved ones that love you may not act rudely while trying to reason with you; however, they are human. They are therefore subject to passionate anger, "exploding" with their emotions . . . because they don't want to see you get hurt or killed.
7. Your loved ones that love you aren't self-seeking, to approve of your unsafe habits because they desire your death, to get an early inheritance. They don't want an early inheritance. They want you . . . alive!
8. Your loved ones that love you aren't easily angered by a minor incident you may have. But they can become furious with you if you're hurt . . . or have a "close call" with death . . . for a major incident. The angry words which might race through their minds could be: *I just knew something like this could happen!*
9. Your loved ones that love you don't remember your unsafe acts "on purpose," to hold them against you in some *family court of law*. They're not interested in "trying you for your crimes" of being unsafe. They are for you . . . not against you.
10. Your loved ones that love you don't rejoice when you're convicted of a safety violation by the company you work for. Rather, they rejoice when you're either *proven "not guilty"* or *pardoned*. They rejoice in good news, such as when you're given a second chance.

Seeing the Workplace as a "Wisdom Center"

● Safety truth:

> ***Ignorance*** *of safety rules is a perfect condition for* ***incidents*** *to flourish.*

Until the company sees its workplace as a "wisdom center," it won't have a work force of wise workers.

The workplace must be not only a place where *work is wrought.*

The workplace must be also a place where *wisdom is taught.*

I believe Wisdom is the master key to making the workplace marvelously safe.

The key mission of the workplace as a "wisdom center" consists of three successive goals in each class of instruction which the company may schedule. They are deliberately designed:

1. To *impress* upon employees the need to embrace wisdom. To embrace wisdom, they'd have to forsake their foolishness (foolish thinking, foolish conduct, foolish attempts, etc.). The company wants them to be wise workers.
2. To *improve* the quality of their working life. A safe working life is a solid necessity for staying alive in the workplace. An unsafe working life is a sure path to death and destruction.
3. To *impart* understanding. What they don't understand can ultimately spell their doom. Injury is the *usual* price for ignorance. Death is the *ultimate* price for ignorance.

Just as a restaurant needs chefs or a school needs teachers, so a wisdom center needs *wisdom teachers/instructors.*

Wisdom teachers/instructors are capable of instructing others in wisdom.

Question: Where can the company procure wisdom instructors for its wisdom center?

Anyone can teach *knowledge.*

Everyone cannot teach *wisdom.*

- Wisdom is not *innate*.
- Wisdom is *imparted*.

Wisdom requires teachers or instructors to impart it to others.

Wisdom teachers can be counselors; but, counselors have to be careful to not seek to impart their own *worldly philosophy* but true *wisdom*.

Wisdom teachers/instructors possess the *gift of wisdom*.

The gift of wisdom is given by God . . . but is not given to all.

Therefore, a person possessing a wisdom gift is a rare treasure . . . on earth.

If the company is wise, it will *hire* a person possessing a wisdom gift . . . especially in the area of workplace safety . . . so that the company *has* a wisdom teacher/instructor for its wisdom center.

A person who's a rare treasure of gifted wisdom has to be *discovered* . . . by the company.

The company must see that "special person" as a *wise investment*.

A wise company makes wise investments.

A Wise O.W.L. in the Workplace

If the company wants its workplace to be a *wisdom center*, then it should begin its search for a *wise owl* right there, in its own backyard.

Seen in this light, the workplace is as a "forest."

The work areas of the workplace are as "trees."

The workers of those work areas are as "birds."

Question: Can the company find a "wise owl" among the "birds?"

Another question: Does a wise O.W.L. exist in the workplace?

Using the word *OWL* as an acronym, I let each letter stand for the following:

One
Who's
Looked for

A wise one who's looked for in the workplace will remain *hidden* if he (or she) doesn't work his wisdom gift.

His wisdom gift in operation is the *sign* that must be seen.

Even if you're searching in a dark place, if a gem isn't sparkling or shining brightly, you may *overlook* it. Similarly, if you look for a wise person in the workplace, if he isn't "shining brightly" or doing his thing, you might overlook him. He has to *demonstrate* his wisdom gift [in the workplace] so that others can *discover* him [in the workplace]. Otherwise, he will be overlooked and others may never know of him.

Here are seven identifying marks of a Wise O.W.L. which to look for among particular persons in the workplace. A Wise O.W.L. is:

1. A *principled* person. He leads a morally clean life.
2. A *productive* person. His life yields good results.
3. A *peaceful* person. He avoids strife . . . when he can.
4. A *people* person. He loves to socialize with others.
5. A *patient* person. He bears with others.
6. A *perceptive* person. He is discerning.
7. A *passionate* person. He is strongly emotional, especially in speech, when he addresses an audience.

All of these seven personal traits allude to the real fact that this is, indeed, *a person of integrity.*

A person of integrity is an upright person who walks in his *integrity.*

Integrity, as I believe, is the *missing key* to safe performance of workers in the workplace.

Integrity is steadfast adherence to something.

If workers steadfastly adhered to the safety rules and regulations of the company, then would they guide themselves safe and sound through their work shift. Their integrity (rigid adherence to safety rules) would *influence* their safe conduct.

Where there is no *integrity* there will be no *influence* within self to do what is right . . . and safe.

SAFETY COUNSEL FOR YOU TO CONSIDER

- The personal incident you *lie about* may be a hidden trap you *lay for* some other unsuspecting employee.
- Don't *race* against time. Instead, *remain* in your safety lane.
- If you *make sure* something is safe, then you won't *mistake* it to be safe.
- What you fail to *recognize* you may *regret*.
- If Safety is no *accident*, then it is an *accomplishment*.
- A *safe moment* must be *multiplied* . . . to have a *safe day*. Just as there are 24 hours in a day, you should have *many* moments of being safe during the day.
- Where there is *indulgence* in unsafe behavior, there will be *incidents*.
- The workplace is not a place to *party* . . . but to *perform* your work safely.
- *Reproof* is *real proof* that you care about someone.
- If you don't *speak up* about a safety incident you know you can lend "valuable information" about, it can *spell* disaster for someone else.
- You cannot *dodge* what you *do not see* coming.
- If you *fake* being safe, you may *find* yourself riding in an ambulance . . . or a hearse.
- When you look at something, make sure you look at it *right*.

3

Wearing E.A.R. Protection: Have Your Hearing!

● Safety truth:

> *Respecting what can kill you can save your life; therefore,* **daredevils** *are* **deathseekers.**

As surely as you have *employment,* you will have *experiences* at the place where you're employed. For this reason, I encourage you to "wear" what I call E.A.R. protection. Using the word *EAR* as an acronym, I let each letter stand for the following:

Experience it.
Analyze it.
Report it.

Working in the workplace is like working *in a laboratory.*
In a laboratory, one conducts experiments.
Experiments produce *experiences.*
Experiences are *analyzed,* to see what can be *found out or learned.*
What is found out or learned is then *reported.*
It is expected of the investigator/researcher to report his findings.

When you have an incident, you have an *experience.*
An experience should be *analyzed,* to see what knowledge or insight can be *acquired* from it.

▶ You should report what you *live through* . . . or experience.
▶ You should share what you *learn* from what happens to you.

Some people "cover up" their incidents (what happen to them) and that for a number of reasons.

When you choose to *hide* your incident, you choose not to *help* someone else.

Reporting your incident is a real step in paving the way for a safe workplace.

Remember, when you have an incident:

1. You *experience* it.
2. You *analyze* it.
3. You *report* it.

You will have your hearing!
You will have your *opportunity to be heard.*
What you have to say *matters.*

It matters because just as prospectors seek to find gold nuggets in rocks, investigators seek to find "gold nuggets" or very valuable information in the "rocks" of your real experience.

- *Investigation* seeks to "solve the mystery" of what may have happened.
- *Interview* is an attempt to glean valuable information from you.
- *Interrogation* sets the platform for pointed questions. Questions must be asked . . . if the "mystery" of what happened is to be solved.

D.E.A.F. Employees: Dealing With Different Kinds of Undesirable Workers

● Safety truth:

A safe act is a **seed** *. . . for the* **harvest** *of your preservation.*

Some employees are what I call D.E.A.F. Using the word *DEAF* as an acronym, I let each letter stand for the following:

Doing
Everything (and)
Anything
For self

There are people in the workplace, who do everything and anything for self. They are selfish workers rather than true team players. Everything and anything they do, they seek to do *for themselves*. Selfish workers can potentially negatively affect a *safe workplace* . . . by virtue of negatively affecting the *safe condition* of coworkers.

18 Undesirable Elements in the Work Environment

1. **"*Narcissists*" in the workplace.** These are *self-loving workers*. They have an excessive regard for their own advantage and interests. They think chiefly of themselves, preferring themselves over their fellow workers. They seek to get all the "best deals" in their work area . . . not caring if their coworkers get the "worst deals." They don't care about heaping up the majority of the work on others. They try to avoid as much "demanding work" as possible, seeking to get out of doing everything and anything that will make them have to put out, sweat, become musty, and very dirty.
2. **"*Crooks*" in the workplace.** These are *greedy workers*. They are money lovers. As money lovers, they're subject to doing evil things in the workplace, for money. For money, they will become unfaithful, to do things they normally wouldn't do. They may even endanger their *coworkers* for their *concentration* on money . . . and getting their hands on some extra money.
3. **"*Self-Proclaimed Stars*" in the workplace.** These are *self-glorifying workers*. They proclaim . . . throughout their work area . . . to be the best in their work area. When others praise them, their superegos are feed enormously. This can induce them to doing "whatever it takes" to remain number one . . . and to "put on a good show." They're driven to retain "first place." This can easily expose them to unnecessarily take risks, so they can "take the cake."

4. ***"Proud Peacocks"* in the workplace.** These are *proud workers*. Knowledge puffs up. It can make a person proud, to the extreme point that he thinks . . . and feels . . . he doesn't need anyone telling him anything. This can include that he thinks he doesn't need anyone telling him what he's doing or how he's doing it, is unsafe. He will get offended by anyone who seems to be trying to "show him up" or make him look like he doesn't know what he's doing . . . when all they may seek to do is ensure he's safe.
5. ***"Abusers"* in the workplace.** These are *abusive workers*. They abuse other workers in the sense they assail others with contemptuous, coarse, or insulting words. They love to revile coworkers. Their verbal abuse can create one of two reactions:
    ▶ They can get a **demoralization** *reaction,* in which the workers are disheartened.
    ▶ They can get a **retaliation** *reaction,* in which the workers return like for like, or evil for evil.

    Abuse undermines team morale. It jeopardizes the safety goal . . . in so many ways. When one worker *abuses* another, he good as *attacks* that worker . . . with the "weapon" of his words.
6. ***"Rebellious Children"* in the workplace.** These are *disobedient workers*. They don't do like the company/superiors want them to do. They do like *they* want to do. Doing like they want to do can mean doing things in a dangerous manner. When they are *uncooperative,* they can be *unsafe*.
7. ***"Spoiled Brats"* in the workplace.** These are *ungrateful workers*. When the company/superiors "spoil" workers, they are running the very high risk of creating "Frankenstein monsters" or spoiled employees, who think they're owed everything they receive. They simply see no reason to thank others for what they feel is owed them . . . or that they feel they deserve. When workers become *ungrateful,* they may become *unsafe* . . . disregarding dangerous conditions as they may turn a deaf ear to given warnings.
8. ***"Villains"* in the workplace.** These are *wicked workers*. They simply don't belong in the workplace, having corrupt practices, seizing any and every opportunity to "get over." They are virtually "no good" to the company or coworkers. They can be the worst troublemakers ever witnessed in the workplace. Some of their most hideous work in the workplace is *sabotage*. They will

sabotage others, for whatever reason. For them, *sabotage* can be *safety violation.*

9. **"*Demons*" in the workplace.** These are *hateful workers.* They try to do a good job at disguising their hatefulness. But if they feel "betrayed" or "wronged," the "real them" will come forth, for everyone to see. They can be the most revengeful, cruel, "doing-their-dirt-on-the-sly" workers in the workplace. They will take their wrath out on anyone either their equal or ranking below them . . . even if it means doing wicked things to endanger the workers they show hate towards. They could care less about the safety or well-being of their coworkers, who they have a problem with.

10. **"*Fortified Citadels*" in the workplace.** These are *unforgiving workers.* If you offend them in a major way, whether by something you say or something you do, they will lock you out of their lives, much like bars keeping others out, as of a city or castle. If you shout warnings to them of imminent danger, in all probability, they will ignore you. Their *ignoring you* can possibly result in their *incident.* Ignored warnings can lead to invited tragedies.

11. **"*Character Assassins*" in the workplace.** These are *slanderous workers.* They slander people with the dark purpose of *injuring* their reputation. Their words are harmful and often untrue, tending to discredit or malign others. Should this "bad news" reach the workers who're slandered, it may preoccupy their minds, thus serving as *mental distractions,* which may potentially result in them getting hurt . . . or possibly killed.

12. **"*Loose Cannons*" in the workplace.** These are *uncontrolled workers.* These workers appear to be beyond control and are potential sources of *unintentional damage.* Unintentional damage can be property damage or human damage. Human damage, of course, is *human injury.*

13. **"*Savage Beasts*" in the workplace.** These are *fierce workers.* They have a savage and violent nature. They are human seeds for workplace violence. They're always "looking for a fight." Fighting in the workplace can result in injury or unintended death.

14. **"*Jealousy Monsters*" in the workplace.** These are *jealous workers.* Whom they're jealous of they *despise.* Particularly, they despise those workers who seek to do good in the workplace. Some

people are jealous of other people's gifts, talents, and uncommon abilities. If their jealousy reaches "maximum overdrive," they'll be driven by their jealousy to thwart the good plans and good intentions of those "do-gooders." Sabotage can also be found in their jealousy arsenal. They may become tempted to "take someone out" . . . by some diabolic means.

15. *"Benedict Arnolds"* **in the workplace.** These are *treacherous workers*. They are traitors to the righteous cause of the company/workers with good ideas. They have self-seeking in their hearts. They will defect to and "hook up with" others who want the cause of righteousness to fail. These treacherous workers will "make a deal" with these kinds of people, wanting to know, *"What's in it for me?"* These traitors are subject to seek to destroy safe conditions of the workplace, to thwart the good plans and good intents of others, which they may have for the workplace, to improve it.

16. *"Daredevils"* **in the workplace.** These are *reckless workers*. They take fearless, foolish chances with their well-being . . . and their very lives. They're known for pulling dangerous stunts in the workplace, not caring for their own safety. They have an overwhelming need to *impress others*. They fearlessly, foolishly risk their own injury or fatality.

17. *"Highlanders"* **in the workplace.** These are *vain or conceited workers*. I call them "highlanders" because they think *more highly* of themselves than they ought to think, in the workplace. In the world of their own hearts, they "see" themselves as being higher than others . . . having higher skills, higher performance, higher pay, etc. They render themselves potential candidates for personal incidents. They always (or most of the time) feel they "have something to prove." Whenever you feel you have something to prove, you may unknowingly place your feet upon the path to a potential incident.

18. *"Playboys/Playgirls"* **in the workplace.** These are *pleasure-loving workers*. They're always seeking to "have a good time" . . . in the workplace. They can be work dodgers, as they stop working to dance or do what they love to do. They are begging for something bad to happen to them. They don't take their work *seriously*. They *play* at every opportunity they get. Their pleasure-seeking ways are actually *invitations for incidents*.

The Abominable S.N.O.W. Man

● Safety truth:

> *Patient workers don't **hurry** their death. They **hold** their life dear.*

I call this kind of employee, whose unsafe way of doing things is an abomination to the company, the abominable S.N.O.W. Man.

Using the word *SNOW* as an acronym, I let each letter stand for the following:

Stubborn
Noncompliant
Overconfident
Worker

Now the company doesn't detest the *person* of whom the employee is.
The company detests the *practices* of the employee, which are unsafe.
What he does . . . not who he is . . . is what makes him an abominable employee to the company.

✎ *Your **unsafe** practices will make you an **undesirable** employee!*

Such an employee is very bad for the workplace.
When it comes to being safe, he is poor in quality.
He is inferior to a safe work environment.
The fact of the matter is: The company hates unsafe habits!

Scaring the Company

This kind of employee scares the company by virtue of making it fear he may get eventually hurt. It is this fear . . . for the employee's safety . . . that may move the company to let the employee go.
The company doesn't see the employee as a *monster*.
Rather, it sees him as a *maximum risk*.

The company will seek to eliminate its fear . . . for the employee . . . by releasing him.

Releasing him isn't an act of *judgment* but an act of *mercy*.

An act of mercy of this nature can make it financially hard for that person.

But it is better for that person that he has it *financially hard* than that he has a *funeral*.

Appearing before the "Judgment Seat" of the Company: How Do You Plead?

◐ Safety truth:

> An incident: If it doesn't take your **life**, then you should take a **lesson** from it.

Counting itself fair, the company will hear your "case" . . . or your incident.

Your *incident* describes your *involvement* in what happened to you.

How do you plead?

If you plead "Guilty," will the company *fire* you or *forgive* you?

If you plead "Not guilty," will the company *believe* you or *disbelieve* you?

If you plead "Guilty," the company will have to *decide on* what to do about you.

If you plead "Not guilty," the company will have to *depend on* two critical things:

1. *Evidence*
2. *Eyewitnesses*

Safety violations are considered by the company to be "crimes." However, every incident isn't the result of a safety violation. That's why the company has to hear your "case."

Your "case" is your incident.

Your incident may contain valuable information of:

- *Unknown dangers* the company will need to address.
- *Unsafe conditions* the company will need to correct.
- *Unguarded things* the company will need to see if it can guard or for what it can put a guard in place.
- *Uncooperative employees* the company will need to examine to determine if they're real threats to the other safe-working employees.

Though you may have a *trial,* the company is after the *truth* . . . of what happened . . . or what you did.

If you're not guilty, then you should not be afraid.

If you're guilty, then you should be afraid!

If you *lie* you may *lose* your job, any way.

If you tell the truth, it may either *help* or *hurt* your chances of remaining employed at that workplace. However, the truth isn't meant for your evil, but your good.

Good ultimately will come out of telling the truth.

Telling the truth is what a person of integrity does.

Called In for Questioning by "The Police"

- Safety truth:

   *You may have never looked at it like this: A **deliberate violation** of safety rules is as good as a **death wish.***

The company has to be "the police" of its own workplace. It has to police its workplace for "criminal activities" or safety violations of its workers.

The company may "call in" certain workers for questioning . . . concerning incidents which they were involved in or innocently witnessed.

The "criminal" or safety violator "the police" may seek is a fellow worker of them called in for questioning.

He sees absolutely nothing wrong with the way he may perform his work. However, the company will want to "weigh" his motives . . . for doing things the way he does them.

Upon investigation, if it's determined an incident was caused by *human error,* then a *human being* will be sought.

A human being who is sought is a *suspect.*

A suspect is one who's suspected of committing a crime. Therefore, the worker who's sought is suspected of committing a "crime" or safety violation.

Notwithstanding, he is innocent until proven guilty.

As innocent until proven guilty, he should know:
▶ An incident requires *investigation.*
▶ Investigation involves *interrogation.*
▶ Interrogation "digs for" *invaluable information.*

Sometimes, workers will "turn themselves in," being the ones who caused the incident.

Oftentimes, workers will not "come forth," for fear of getting into trouble or getting the boot. They don't wish to lose their job. So they keep quiet . . . about their involvement in an incident.

As far as the company is concerned, if one doesn't "come clean," then he will get into trouble. But some workers aren't so willing to take that chance. So they go on in the workplace . . . not as *fugitives,* but as *faces* unidentified for incidents.

As long as the incident is an "open case," the suspect will be sought.

But when the incident is declared a "closed case," the suspect will no longer be "hunted."

As long as he doesn't *step forward,* he will *stay a mystery* . . . to the company.

The company, in all likelihood, won't *put out* a "warrant for his arrest." But it will *put on file* the incident . . . for future reference.

Punishing "Partners in Crime"

When a worker aids a coworker in committing a "crime" or safety violation, the company considers them "partners in crime."

As "partners in crime," they will be sought.

If found they will be *convicted*.

If convicted (of a "crime" or safety violation), the company will then determine *their* punishment.

The employee who's proud in heart, is a rebel against the company and its safety program, and therefore is an abomination to the company. He will *definitely* be punished . . . if caught.

Also, the coworker who aids that "criminal" or safety violator will *deservingly* be punished.

He can be punished for his *involvement,* not necessarily his *commitment* of the crime.

Purging the "Body" of Workers

The "body" of workers in the workplace can be purged of the practice of safety violation by two crucial elements: love and commitment.

▶ When workers *love* themselves, they will not do anything to endanger themselves.
▶ When workers *learn to be committed* to Safety, they will consistently deliberately avoid safety violation.

Ultimately, a safe workplace depends on the safe performance of its workers.

Its workers are the key to keeping the workplace safe.

Keeping the workplace safe is the responsibility . . . and duty . . . of employees.

Employees shouldn't allow the *routine* of work to desensitize them to the *real dangers* of work.

Work shouldn't be your main concern.

Working safe should be your main concern.

Safety Lessons: An "Unteachable Student"

● Safety truth:

> Question: *If you don't want to **die**, why would you **dare** to die by taking foolish risks?*

If it is one thing I've learned in all my working years, it is this:

> *If you try to **reason with** a foolish worker, he will only **despise** the wisdom of your words.*

I regard my mouth as a "school."
The words which my mouth speaks are as "lessons."
The person who is listening to me speak I regard as a "student."
When you *listen* to people speak, you can *learn* from them.

If you have something to say to someone pertaining to safety and that person doesn't care to hear it, you should recognize that person as an "unteachable student."
An unteachable student cannot learn.
He cannot learn because he *refuses* to learn.
Because he refuses to learn, he *rejects* the safety lessons he could possibly learn.
Fellow workers who're *unteachable* students allow themselves to be *unsafe* workers.
Unsafe workers are not all foolish workers.

3 Basic Types of Workers in the Workplace

As I have identified over my working years, there are three basic types of workers in the workplace. They are:

1. **Scornful workers.** They are foolish workers. They hate to learn anything they think they don't need to know. So they won't listen . . . to you. That's why when you speak to them, they scorn what you say. They belittle it. They see no real value in your words. These types of workers can only learn by *punishment*. Punishment for them must be dealt out by the company . . . which isn't imitated by them. If they won't listen to you, then they'll either *listen to* the company or *lose* their job.
2. **Naïve workers.** They aren't necessarily scornful; however, they can be foolish. They have a tendency to *follow the lead* of

scornful workers. But once they see what happens to scornful workers who're punished, they're made to "see the light" . . . and the error of their working ways. Usually, all it takes for them *to learn* is having scornful workers made *object lessons* to them . . . by the company. They don't wish to experience the *wrath* of the company. The company *strikes fear* into their hearts by what it does to rebellious workers.

3. **Wise workers.** They are *good listeners.* As good listeners, they hear and heed instruction. Because they hear and heed instruction, they receive knowledge. Because they receive knowledge, they become *wiser.* They genuinely respect the life principle that learning is a never-ending process. They recognize they can *learn* as long as they *live.* While scornful workers and naïve workers can be the *problem workers* of the workplace, wise workers are the *pride and joy* of the workplace.

Too Proud to Listen

● Safety truth:

> *The employee who **puts his trust** in machines **puts his life** in danger.*

When a worker is too proud to listen, he paves the way for his own destruction or personal ruin.

Though you do your best to *reach* him, you cannot *rescue* him; only *report* him.

If you forbear to report him . . . for whatever reason . . . you allow him to continue on that path to destruction.

When your *friendly reminders* become *frightful warnings,* a fatality just may be around the corner.

↯ *Pride can be a prelude to one's death!*

You are then confronted with a choice: Clear your conscience or be "killed" by it.

It is better to report the proud worker who won't heed your repeated warnings than forbear to report him, learn of his death, and be strongly tempted to say, "I didn't know anything about it."

If you fail to report him and he ends up dead, your conscience will haunt you . . . for the rest of your natural life.

You knew about it . . . but you didn't report it.
Why??

Carefully consider these thoughts:

- The proud worker you forbear to *report,* the fatal outcome you may *regret.*
- It is not *betrayal* to report such a one. But it is *being concerned.*
- You may *lose* a friend, but he won't *lose* his life.
- What you can courageously *say* to a very proud worker may actually *save* his life.

You have to understand that when the foolishness of a proud worker *perverts* his way of doing things, his heart will rage against the company . . . when the company addresses the matter. Even if he gets angry at the company for caring about his safety, if you don't report him, he will remain headed for self-destruction. It becomes a real matter of life and death.

How to Avoid Becoming a "Victim" of Incidents: A Simple Solution

● Safety truth:

> *If you enter the workplace with your body **awake** but your mind **asleep**, you're nothing more than a walking incident . . . just waiting to happen.*

What I mean by becoming a "victim" of incidents is always finding yourself in incidents.

There is a simple solution: Give the company your *heart.*

Your heart is where *submission* takes place.

When you submit to the company's safety rules, you will observe its safe-working ways.

The simple solution is submission.

Learn to do things the safe way.

The safe way isn't necessarily *your* way.

Your way should be the safe way!

When you submit to the company's safety rules, you will make its safe practices your safe practices.

But, it takes *humility* to submit.

▶ The humble worker is the one who'll **submit to** the company's safety rules.
▶ The proud worker is the one who'll **rebel against** the company's safety rules.

You don't have to be a "victim" of incidents!

Granted, things happen in the workplace. However, you can take steps to *at least* minimize what may happen to you.

The safety goal of *zero incidents* can seem far-fetched, but it is not altogether impossible.

What is not impossible is possible.

What is possible is attainable.

What is attainable has to be consistently worked towards.

Workers have to be earnest in their efforts to establish a safe workplace . . . and a safe work record.

A Far-Reaching Question for You: "What are you doing?"

● Safety truth:

> ***Loving*** *your neighbor is also* ***looking out*** *for your fellow worker.*

On the one hand, doing things the right way is doing them the safe way. Doing them the safe way will *preserve* you in the workplace.

On the other hand, doing things the wrong way is doing them the unsafe way. Doing them the unsafe way will *overthrow* you. It will bring about your downfall or destruction in the workplace.

Here is a far-reaching question for you to seriously consider: *"What are you doing?"*

I ask you this particular question for two reasons:

1. The practice of doing things the right way will bring you *honor* in the workplace. The company and your superiors and coworkers will respect you for being a safe worker. A safe worker is sought to do safety talks.
2. The practice of doing things the wrong way will bring you *dishonor* in the workplace. Dishonor is disgrace. The company and your superiors and coworkers will tend to look down on you for being an unsafe worker. An unsafe worker is a very poor influence on greenhorn workers. So in all likelihood, he won't be chosen as a trustworthy trainer.

So what are you doing?
Are you doing safe work . . . or unsafe work?
It really matters.
For that it really matters, your superior and coworkers should know what you're doing.

Doing Something That May Lead to a "Dead End"

There is a way of doing something that can seem right and safe, but it may lead you to a "dead end."
A "dead end" to which I refer is a *fatality*.
A fatality doesn't just happen. It is an *effect*.
An effect has a *cause*.
Thus, a fatality has a cause . . . a fatal cause.
A cause can be one's way of doing something.
One's way of doing something can prove to be dangerous . . . and deadly.

> ✥ Safety **preached** to the workers but not **practiced** by them is a futile sermon!

Whatever you do, do it to the glorious cause of safety!
Safety depends on you!
You are the secret to a safe workplace!
Therefore, you are *very important* . . . to the company's safety goal!
But you have to *know* you're very important to its vision . . . of being a safe workplace.
So **know** it and **grow** with it!

An Ancient Safety Secret: A Wise Council

● Safety truth:

> **Embarrassment** *for being unsafe can sometimes be as much a positive tool as* **encouragement** *to be safe.*

A safety council is not much good or won't be that effective if it's not a *wise council*.

A wise council consists of *wise council members*.

Wise council members are *wise persons*.

Wise persons can come up with *wise counsel*.

▶ Wisdom is the key to *safety*.

▶ Wise counsel is the key to *safe workers*.

Safety council members must not only *know* what is unsafe; they must also *understand* the nature of and the set of existing circumstances surrounding an incident.

Safety council members must be *private investigators* of workplace incidents.

As such, they cannot afford to count on *information* alone.

They must also obtain *insight* from others, who may hold "clues" to what actually happened . . . and why it happened.

Safety council members must be trained to be *mystery solvers*.

An *unsolved mystery* of what happened could prove to be an *unrecognized danger* that is not taken care of . . . and that could come back to haunt the safety council, should another worker suffer the same fate as one originally did.

Obviously, the company has to be *wise* in selecting members to its safety council.

Anyone can set on the safety council; but, not everyone is a *wise person*.

A wise person operates in *practical wisdom* . . . not *personal opinions*.

Wherefore, an unwise person will prove to be a disappointment to the safety council, and will do it injustice in its righteous cause of safety.

The "FBI" of the Workplace

The safety council is the "FBI" of the workplace. It is an agency of the company responsible for investigating violation of safety laws the company establishes and enforces.

As can be seen, the safety council has a very serious responsibility. That's why it cannot afford to have on its seat unwise persons.

Unwise persons on the safety council are prone to *judgment* . . . or judging other workers . . . rather than being for *justice* . . . wanting to justify the workers, if at all possible.

A *wise council* is a *wonderful part* of the workplace.

As the safety council of the workplace, it has three primary safety objectives:

1. Building a safe workplace through wise counsel.
2. Instilling in the workers the belief that a safe workplace becomes strong through their day-to-day common-sense decisions and actions.
3. Filling the workplace with workers who really care and are responsible. As safety council members, they have a duty to detect and report workers who really don't care and are irresponsible.

A *person* on the safety council should possess a *passion* for safety.

Safety should be championed by him more than anyone else who's not on the safety council.

Safety should not only *matter* to him. It should also *motivate* him . . . to continue his most honorable quest for a safe workplace.

Bringing Back the "Strays": Death Seekers

● Safety truth:

> A worker who **strays from** the right way of doing things eventually will be **found dead.**

It can be a most frightening thought.

It should be a most frightening thought.

When you see a worker straying from the right way of doing things, you should say something . . . not turn a blind eye to it . . . for fear of that fellow worker being found dead.

You simply must get into the habit of bringing back the "strays" . . . workers who stray from doing their job the right way.

The right way is the safe way.
The safe way presents NO opportunities for incidents.
Incidents can be fatal.
Fatal is never good.
Fatal means more than loss of a worker. It also means loss of a human life.

Workers who stray from doing their job the right and safe way become what I call "death seekers."
Death seekers seek death.
These *unwary* workers seek death . . . without even knowing it.
They're on a *death quest . . . and don't know it.*
You bring back the "strays" by saying something to them; and, if they refuse to hear and heed your words, then you report them to your superior.
Do every thing decently and in order.
Do your part!

Snitching in the Workplace: Friend or Foe?

There is the sensitive matter of snitching in the workplace.
In the workplace, people "snitch on" people.
People who're "snitched on" feel *betrayed.*
Betrayed, they despise the betrayer.
The betrayer undoubtedly has *his motive.*
His motive is what should be placed under the microscope.

People in the workplace want to know if you're their "friend" or their "foe."
The way they see it, if you're their "friend," you won't snitch on them; but, if you're their "foe," you will snitch on them.
But this is *their* viewpoint.
Now let's look at *another* viewpoint—one of justice and moral right.
Snitching is turning informer.
An informer is a person who *informs against* someone.
That person discloses confidential or incriminating information to an authority.

If you happened to witness a fellow worker commit a safety violation or some unsafe act and you *reported it,* does that really make you a snitch?

See, it's *your motive* for reporting it that holds the answer to that question.

The real question is: *Are you a snitch or a concerned co-worker?*
- A *snitch* will report it because he wants that person to get into trouble.
- A *concerned co-worker* will report it because he wants that person to be responsible . . . and safe.

In the workplace, you should be a concerned co-worker before being a friend.

A friend may not report it, but a concerned coworker will.

If your "snitching" will help protect someone or save someone's life, then being labeled a "snitch" by them shouldn't really bother you.

You should be satisfied to know that they'd better not *DO IT AGAIN!*

You can be a 'hero' and be called a 'bad guy' at the same time!

"The House of Representatives"

Safety truth:

> The workplace is not a **playground,** but a **production facility.** Children don't belong there; only adults.

I call the workers in the workplace "the house of representatives."

I call them that especially because they're expected of the company to *represent safety.*

To represent safety, they have to be safe workers.

Safe workers take safety seriously.

They not only represent the very company they work for. They also represent the working people of the world.

If you're an employee, then you're a member of the "house of representatives."

As a member of the "house of representatives," you should regard yourself as a *representative.*

A representative is a *responsible worker.*
A responsible worker is a *really safe worker.*

As a representative, you should be in conjunction with the rest of the safe workers of the workplace, in seeking to get "safety bills" passed.

Whenever you see something unsafe or think of something that will improve safety of the workplace, you should definitely try to have a "safety bill" about it "passed"—with the help of your fellow safe workers. In the way of safety, the company is always looking for:

- *New information*
- *New insights*
- *New ideas*
- *New inventions*
- *New innovations*

If you're among the safe workers in the workplace and you don't *speak up,* then what chance does the workplace itself has to be safe continually?

You're not only a *valuable employee* to the company.

You're also a *voice for safety* in the workplace.

"The Safety Senate"

- Safety truth:

    Improving *your safe conduct should always be more important to you than* ***impressing*** *others.*

I call the safety council "the safety senate."

I call the safety council members the "safety senators" of the workplace.

They are the very ones the general manager himself convenes with in special safety meetings on a regular basis.

As "the safety senate," the safety council has the function of amending "safety bills" or safety rules. A "representative" or common worker cannot do this. He can *advise* about changes he may consider necessary, but he cannot *amend* safety rules, as set forth by the company and its safety council.

"The house of representatives" (common workers) will want "the safety senate" (safety council) to agree to pass the safety bills they want to see enacted in the workplace. However, "the safety senate" (safety council) can *veto* the proposed "safety bills," if there's no genuine need for them.
▶ "The house of representatives" presents the **petitions** *of safety.*
▶ "The safety senate" possesses the **power** *to enforce safety rules.*

Sense "the house of representatives" are the *eyes* in the workplace . . . doing the actual work, seeing everything that actually happens . . . "the safety senate" should be the *ears* . . . to listen to their safety concerns.

If the both can *learn* to work together, they can *lead* a safe workplace.

"The Safety Congress"

● Safety truth:

> *If you don't **remember** the safety rules, you will **regret** it . . . in time.*

Together, "the house of representatives" and "the safety senate" make up what I call "the safety congress."

"The safety congress" serves the purpose of coming up with safety concerns and ideas and writing up "safety bills." They may even argue against each other and then vote whether to pass those safety bills. However, the safety bills go to the general manager for final approval. Also, "the safety congress" can declare war on unsafe practices, unsafe conditions, unsafe employees, etc. It is purpose-driven to make and maintain a safe place to work.

A good workplace is the goal of a good company.
A good company has a good reputation.
A good reputation for being a safe workplace should be chosen over great profits, and being esteemed by the employees should be more valuable to the company than being wealthy.

*A good company to work for cares more about its **workers** than its **wealth**.*

That may sound very hard to believe; nevertheless, it's true.

Perhaps that may explain . . . in part . . . why so many companies aren't good to work for.

The "Day of Battle": Preparing the H.O.R.S.E.

● Safety truth:

> *Whether foolish or honest, a mistake can cost a **limb** . . . or a **life**.*

I refer to every workday as a "day of battle."

A "day of battle" is a workday wherein employees must battle to stay safe . . . throughout the entire work shift.

They must battle:

- To stay *focused* . . . on what they're doing.
- To stay *fearful* . . . of what can harm them.
- To stay *free* . . . of unsafe actions and unsafe areas.
- To stay *firm* . . . in purpose to perform their work safely.

Every workday, to win the "day of battle," they must prepare what I call the H.O.R.S.E.

Using the word *HORSE* as an acronym, I let each letter stand for the following:

Highest
Objective (to be)
Responsible (and)
Safe
Employees

At the beginning of each work shift, the "person in charge" of the on-shift crew should prepare the H.O.R.S.E. or the highest objective to be responsible and safe employees.

Employees then must prepare [themselves] to "fight for" this highest objective. They have to continually bear in mind both the production goal and the quality goal come second to the safety goal. They must "ride" the H.O.R.S.E. against their "day of battle" . . . to win a safe work shift.

They should know that safety is no *accident*, but that it is an *acquisition*. A safe work shift must be acquired . . . by their diligent efforts.

Their diligent efforts to keep safe will reward them with the "high prize" of a safe work shift.

A safe work shift is "good news" to the crew and to the company for that it represents the wonderful fact that no one got hurt . . . or killed.

It's a Matter of Respect!

Safety truth:

> The employee who works safe **respects** the company and its safety concern. But the employee who is unsafe in his work **despises** the company and its safety concern.

Safe workers are compliant with the company.
Compliance is a common proof of respect.
▶ **Respect** is what the company *expects* from its employees.
▶ **Respect** is what employees *expect* from the company.
Unsafe workers are noncompliant with the company.
Noncompliance is a common proof of despite.
The company has people working for it, who either respect or despise it and its safety program.

What one *respects* he *responds to.*
What one *despises* he *doesn't care for.*

Safe workers respect their body parts and their very lives.
The converse is also true: Unsafe workers despise their body parts and their very lives.
What you **refuse** *to* **respect** *can* **ruin** *you . . . body-wise or life-wise.*

*What you **despise** can **destroy** you . . . if it possesses dangerous potential.*

🖖 *Respect can be a real life-saver!*

A Principle to Preserve Not Just Your Job . . . But Also Your Life

● Safety truth:

> *The safe way of the safe worker is to **avoid** unsafe practices. The employee who keeps his safe way of doing things **preserves** his job . . . and his life.*

Indeed, this preservation principle is one that all employees should know and unfailingly apply in their everyday work life.

When you *avoid* unsafe practices you *avert* unexpected incidents.

Safety violators run the very high risk of losing not just their jobs but also their very lives.

Their very lives are endangered [to some degree] every time they violate a safety rule or regulation.

When you *leave* the safe way of doing things, you risk *losing* something.

- A *limb* could be lost.
- A *life* could be lost.
- A *lot* could be lost.

It's always better to be safe than sorry!

It's always better to think about what you're doing *now* than to think about what you will be doing *later* . . . *or when you get off work.*

🖖 *Safety is the solemn responsibility of every employee!*

The Joy Factor: Being Glad for Being Safe

● Safety truth:

> The safe worker who faithfully does what is right will receive ***joy***. But the unsafe worker who makes a practice of safety violation will receive ***judgment***.

Joy can come from simply being safe and not being involved in an incident that's caused by unsafe action. But "judgment" or decreed punishment by the company, comes to them that insist on doing things the unsafe way.

You are *happy* when you're not *held responsible* for something that unfortunately happens.

When you're *innocent* of an *incident*, you feel good on the inside . . . and relieved.

↳ *Joy is a just reward for being safe!*

A workplace full of safe workers can quickly become a joyous place to work. Joy is a secret of a delightful workplace. Happy workers normally have better productivity results. When workers are safe, joy can come as the consequence of:

- Reaching the *safety goal.*
- Reaching the *quality goal.*
- Reaching the *production goal.*

Joy can be the consequence of *team effort.* When workers accomplish something together, it has the wonderful tendency to make them rejoice together.

Joy is a *wonderful* experience.
Joy can also be a *work* experience.

SAFETY COUNSEL FOR YOU TO CONSIDER

- When you *envy* unsafe workers, you *endanger* yourself. You want to do like they do. To do like they do is to do the wrong thing. Be different by doing the right thing.
- Being safe has its *rewards*. Being unsafe has its *regrets*. Be safe and you will be glad you did!
- Don't let your *feelings* impair your *focus*.
- If you're not *reproved*, your unsafe act may be *repeated*.
- Your *mind* is far more important than your *muscles!*
- If you won't be *safe,* you will be *sorry!* Don't deceive yourself.
- The company can only *protect* you according to your willingness to *practice* its safety laws.
- When you *daydream,* you *disconnect* from what's really going on around you.
- If you're *playing,* there's a good chance you're not *playing it safe.*
- Your *perception* of things [in the workplace] affects your *performance* [in the workplace].
- The workplace requires *communication* . . . and *common sense.*
- What you don't *understand,* don't *undertake.*
- Because you *can be* safe, the company *commands* you to be safe.

4

Wearing "Wisdom Gloves": Handle Safety Matters Wisely!

● Safety truth:

> *The employee who* **heeds** *the company's safety instructions will* **handle** *safety matters accordingly.*

As an employee, you will encounter *safety matters* in the workplace . . . at some point of your work shift. However, the real question is: *How do you handle them?*

The real answer to that is: *The very way the company* **instructed** *you to handle them.*

A worker without safety instruction is a sure incident.

A sure incident can be either an *injury* or a *fatality*.

A fatality just may cause the company to consider the real possibility of whether it failed to give the dead worker *proper instruction on being safe*.

Proper instruction on being safe is for the worker's *protection*.

Protection requires more than mere personal protective equipment. It also requires practical knowledge.

Practical knowledge is so important that for its lack employees can be injured or killed.

What I call "wisdom gloves" are *wise actions*.

Wise actions are the products of *wise decisions*.

Wise decisions are made by a *wise person*.
A wise person will make a *wise worker*.
A wise worker will handle safety matters wisely.

Look Ahead!

● Safety truth:

> *The wise employee* **considers** *the possibility of what might happen should he execute a certain action; but the naïve employee* **continues** *with his work performance, only to regret it.*

A safe worker is a wise worker.
A wise worker has to be prudent.
To be prudent is to *foresee* the danger and prepare to avoid it. The real fact of the matter is that there are dangers or conditions just right for incidents which you can *see before they happen . . . to you.*
You have to consider the possibility of what could happen to you . . . if you followed a certain course of action.

A naïve worker will not consider the possibility of what could happen to him, so he simply goes on with his plans to perform his work and doesn't foresee the danger ahead of him and suffers for it.

⚡ *Incidents that can be* **anticipated** *can be* **avoided!**

To ensure a safe workplace, the company doesn't merely need *practical* workers. It needs *prudent* workers.
Prudent workers *look ahead . . . of what they're doing.*
Looking ahead allows them to "see" what may potentially happen . . . to them.
The prudent worker will not *continue.*
He will stop to *consider . . . the possibility of what may happen.*
He's a careful observer in his immediate work area. He keeps one eye on his *work* and another eye on his *workplace.*
He keeps himself aware of his surroundings and therefore is aware of developing circumstances and conditions in his immediate work area.

Keys to Keeping You Safe: Be Wise to Use Them!

● Safety truth:

> *The employee who **trusts** in his heart to keep himself safe and therefore **tries** to be safe . . . without honoring company safety rules . . . is a foolish worker. But the employee who works according to company safety rules, he will be kept safe.*

The safety instructions the company gives you are keys to keeping you safe. So be wise to use them!

Understand that you can be safe *only for yourself.*

You can try to *look out* for others, but you cannot *live* others' lives . . . for them. They must live their own lives. This also includes the fact that they have to work safe *for themselves.*

Work safety is first and foremost an individual responsibility.

An individual responsibility belongs to each individual worker.

Each individual worker is to first *learn* to be safe; then second, *look out* for his or her fellow worker. When every worker has learned to be safe and to look out for the other, then the responsibility becomes a *collective responsibility.*

The *establishment* and *enforcement* of safety rules are proof that the company cares about you.

You should honor the company's safety rules on these grounds alone.

The company wants you to be *safe* . . . so that it and your family won't be *sorry.*

If you happen to see other workers failing to use these keys to keeping safe, remember that you don't have to do the same, or adopt their rebellious attitude.

You be safe!

You be a safe worker!

You be a shining example of work safety . . . in the workplace!

Code R.E.D.

● Safety truth:

> *The employee who **forsakes** the safe way of doing things **finds** correction to be grievous to him; and the employee who hates to be corrected will became dead to the company.*

There is a serious situation with employees in the workplace, which I call Code R.E.D.

Using the word *RED* as an acronym, I let each letter stand for the following:

Real
Employee
Dilemma

There is a real employee dilemma in the workplace where safety is concerned. Some employees who turn away from doing their jobs the right and safe way, may be *punished* for the purpose of improving or reforming their ways and means of doing their work. Unfortunately, among this "corrected" group are sometimes found grieved persons who *take offense* to the disciplinarian action they receive.

Retaliation is inevitable.

They may seek to retaliate against the company by becoming "dead" to the company's safety program. When this happens, they will "go through the motions" of being safe "in public," or when others are around; but they will revert to their unsafe working ways "in private," or when no one else is around.

The employee who becomes "dead" to the company's safety program becomes "dead" to the company. This means the company's hope of that person will perish.

As the gardener will prune his plant by cutting off dead branches, the company just may "prune the plant" or workplace by "cutting off" or getting rid of "dead branches" or workers who're "dead" to it.

It is, indeed, a Code R.E.D. situation.

A Wise Master Builder: Every Workplace Should Have One

● Safety truth:

> *A **wise** general manager will build a safe workplace; however, a general manager who is **foolish** will destroy the possibility of a safe workplace.*

A wise general manager who builds a safe workplace is a *wise master builder.*
A wise master builder is an *architect.*
An architect builds by a *blueprint.*
Similarly, a wise general manager is what I call a "safety architect."
As a safety architect, he will build a safe workplace by a "blueprint" or masterful plan of action.
A masterful plan of action can be "drawn up" with the help of his chief staff.

Building a safe workplace is by far no easy feat to accomplish. Nevertheless, it is *very possible.*
It will require the general manager's:

● Direct focus
● Diligent effort
● Dog-like tenacity
● Dual strength of *passion* and *people* (to help him)

He may *conceive* the vision [of a safe workplace] but he will most definitely need others to *carry* the vision to completion. He not only will need the help of a *safety council.* Also, he will need the help of a *safe group of workers.*

Just as it takes a sports team to win a game and not just the coach, it takes a "team" of workers for the general manager to "coach." Therefore, he is the "safety coach."

He can have his staff (which may consist of assistant general manager, safety director, assistant safety director, superintendents, and general foremen) to serve as his various "coordinators."

But his "quarterbacks" are his supervisors, who work "on the field" with the "team" of workers.

When everyone is doing his job safety-wise, "winning the game" or attaining the safety goal becomes a remarkable possibility that should be preserved by all.

Remember the T.I.T.A.N.S.!

When a single workplace excels in safety, it ends up in the industrial spotlight. The eyes of other workplaces will be on that particular safe workplace. They may very well "scout" not necessarily for *talent*, but definitely for *terrific methods* of workplace safety. They will want to know exactly what is that safe workplace *doing [or practicing]* to be safe.

Using the word *TITANS* as an acronym, I let each letter stand for the following:

Team (that is)
Inspired
Talented
All-star
Noble (and)
Safety

A safe workplace has a safe group of workers.
A safe group of workers is what I call the T.I.T.A.N.S.
The T.I.T.A.N.S. has five safety success secrets which other steel mills need to know and humbly adopt. They are as follows:

1. They are an *inspired team*. The "safety coach" or general manager continually devises new "plays" or ways of inspiring his "team" of workers.
2. They are a *talented team*. The general manager believes in them and they believe in themselves. They believe they have what it takes . . . to be a safe workplace. They firmly believe they got "the right stuff." That alone gives them a wonderful sense of pride.

3. They are an *all-star team*. Every "player on the team" or worker in the workplace is considered a *valuable worker*. A valuable worker is expected to have the good reputation for being a safe worker. Every worker strives to be a safe worker.
4. They are a *noble team*. As such, they have . . . and show . . . high concern for workplace safety. They don't take their safety lightly. It is very important to them; and, they want safety to be very important to other workplaces.
5. They are a *safety team*. They see themselves as the ones to represent a safe workplace, and be proud pioneers in the same. Safety is their common goal, which they strive together, to reach. With them, *striving* for the safety goal isn't enough. They employ the use of *strategizing* to realize their safety goal.

Remember, a safe workplace is spearheaded by the safety coach. The safety coach is the wise general manager who leads an inspired, talented, all-star, noble, and safety team.

As a wise general manager, he's a wise master builder.

Notwithstanding, interesting to note is the fact that he isn't the one who laid the safety foundation. Those who preceded him did. He simply builds upon the safety foundation that has already been laid. But, he has to *take heed* how he builds a safe workplace thereupon.

A *ready* builder must also be a *responsible* builder.

A *responsible* builder gets *remarkable* results!

A Remedy for a Rebellious Workplace

● Safety truth:

> *There are many incidents because of the safety-violation* **problem** *of a workplace. But a wise leader will* **prolong** *its safe condition.*

Where there is a safety-violation problem, there is a *rebellious workplace*.

A rebellious workplace has *rebellious workers*.

Rebellious workers practice safety violation.

Safety violation is the *mother of many incidents*.

This is one of the chief reasons why a workplace must have a *wise leader*.

A wise leader *knows and understands* what must be done . . . to have a safe workplace, and has the force of will the prevailing times require.

He knows and understands that for a safety record to be *protected*, the safe condition of that workplace must be *prolonged*.

A wise leader is a *strong* leader.
A strong leader is the remedy for a rebellious workplace.
A strong leader doesn't have to be an *oppressor*.
But he does have to be an *organizer*.
He must be capable of organizing his workplace, to produce the most favorable conditions for safety while maximizing production efficiency.

A strong leader has the *boldness* to correct rebellious workers.
Rebellious workers don't *intimidate* him.
He sees himself as a "man on a mission."
That mission is a safety mission.
The workers who the general manager can correct, they can be *spared*.
But the workers who he cannot correct, they must be considered *spoiled*.

Naturally, there's no hope for what is spoiled. The only thing to do with it is get rid of it. The workers who the general manager cannot correct he must get rid of. This, of course, will leave a remnant of workers who're humble, malleable, and capable of carrying out safety instruction, as administered by the company command.

> *Just as the majority of incidents are **allowed**, that same majority can be equally **avoided**!*

Work safety is not a *walk in the park*. Instead, it is a *work to be performed*.

It is *common* work, but at the same time it is *very important* work. Any worker can do this kind of work. Every worker should esteem it as the most important work to be continually accomplished in the workplace.

The Power to Make the Company Look Good or Bad: Who Wields It?

● Safety truth:

> *The employee who keeps the safety rules is a wise worker who **shines** in the workplace; but the employee who is a member of a gang of rebellious workers **shames** the company he works for.*

The plain truth is that every employee wields the power to make the company look either good or bad.

It only takes *one stain* to ruin a shirt or dress.

It only takes *one employee* or *one group of employees* to ruin the good image of a company.

Being unsafe is one of the best ways to make the company you work for look bad. A bad safety record will make any company look bad, for that matter.

But, a bad safety record is *redeemable*.

That workplace can turn things around . . . if it has the *right people*.

The right people:

- Take safety *seriously*
- Seek to be safe *tirelessly*
- Strive to make a comeback *determinedly*
- Get themselves together *personally*

They firmly believe in themselves that they have the tools to get the job done.

However, tools do not use themselves. They require *skillful hands*.

Therefore, it takes workers who're *skillful at being safe* to turn the tide of unfortunate events.

Skillful at being safe is a praiseworthy phrase which describes those that *know how* to be safe.

Being *skillful* is *knowing how* to use something or do something.

Safety Gem: A Matter of the Heart

● Safety truth:

> The employee who always respects the safety rules will be **mighty glad** he does; but the employee who hardens his heart will become **mischievous** in job matters.

Not all employees abide by the company's safety rules.
The company's safety rules are *enforceable laws*.
Enforceable laws are the responsibility of *people of power*.
People of power wield the authority to *take action* . . . *against* safety-rule violation.

But what I want to place under the microscope is *a matter of the heart*.
There are employees who *harden their heart* against the will of the company, where safety is concerned. Such is the case when employees are *tempted* to take shortcuts. Being tempted to take shortcuts is no safety violation of the heart. Nevertheless, it:

1. *Presents* them with **temptation.**
2. *Poses* them with a **tough choice.**

The employee who yields to the temptation to take a shortcut hardens his heart against the will of the company.
It is a matter of the heart.
It is a decision made in the secret chamber of the heart, where the employee "takes counsel" with himself.
The *exercise* of the will is dependent upon the *experience* of the heart.
The heart holds the key to unlock either the employee's *submission to* or *rebellion against* the company's will.

> ཡ *The employee who **respects** safety rules increases his chances to **remain alive** in his place of employment!*

The employee who hardens his heart against the will of the company becomes mischievous in the workplace. He finds himself doing things he shouldn't be doing. He finds himself turning from the path of respecting safety rules to turning to the path of "walking on the wild side" . . . in the workplace. Though probably unaware, he will "sow" seeds of unsafe conduct, only to "reap" a harvest of incidents.

A Simple Secret to Staying Safe

● Safety truth:

> *The employee who does the right thing will be* **safe;** *but the employee who is perverse in his ways of doing things will be* **sure to perish.**

The company wants you—its valuable employee—to stay safe.

To stay safe, you have to do the right thing . . . *continually.*

No sooner than you *relax* your vigilance, you may *run into* an incident.

At any time you step from underneath your umbrella while in the rain, you will get wet or get hit with the rain.

At any time you step from beneath the "umbrella" of doing the right thing while in the line of work, you will get hit with an incident.

Doing the right thing is *so simple.*

It is so simple that any and every employee can do it.

But the mysterious missing piece to the safety puzzle doesn't lie within its *simplicity* but rather its *consistency.*

An *inconsistent* worker who works safe will find himself in an *incident.*

At some point, he chooses to *pervert* his way of doing things.

The perversion to which I refer is a *change* . . . from safe practice to unsafe practice.

Unsafe practice is a sure "ticket" for the "game" of incidents.

The "game" of incidents presents the powerful reality that no one really wins.

Despicable Me!

● Safety truth:

> The employee who **ignores** discipline despises himself; but the employee who heeds correction by the company gains understanding, and thereby **improves** his attitude and actions.

If you ignore disciplinarian action that's dealt out by the company for safety violation or such, then you despise yourself. But if you heed correction by the company you will gain understanding.

The understanding you gain from company correction is a real key to improving yourself as a good worker.

A good worker has a good attitude and good actions.

Don't be a despicable employee!

A despicable employee doesn't appreciate the company's concern for his safety and personal well-being.

Such a person lacks self-value considerably.

☞ *Where there is lack of **self-value** there is real possibility of **self-destruction!***

Here are some self-improvement keys to being a good worker:

1. Always be willing to *listen.*
2. Always be willing to *learn.*
3. Always be willing to *look at a different perspective.*
4. Always be willing to *lose a bad habit.*
5. Always be willing to *lead by example.*
6. Always be willing to *let go of past mistakes.*
7. Always be willing to *lighten your load of others' expectations of you.*
8. Always to be willing to *live a humble yet honorable life.*

Correction is proof the company cares about you.

Correction heeded has the precious reward of understanding gained.

Understanding gained will prove to be a "wellspring of life" in the workplace to you.

Value correction!
Correction corrects your focus . . . on what's right . . . and safe . . . and acceptable to the company.

Quest for the S.P.E.A.R.

● Safety truth:

> When **unsafe employees** *multiply, safety violation increases; but the* **safe employees** *will witness their downfall in the workplace.*

Workplace wisdom is employed in *warfare* . . . to protect the workplace and to preserve its safe condition.

A **spear** is a *weapon*.

Using the word *SPEAR* as an acronym, I let each letter stand for the following:

Safety
Principles (for)
Employees (to)
Always
Remember

Here are the safety principles I want you to always remember—in the line of doing your work:

- *Distraction is simply broken focus.* If you can remain focused . . . on what you're doing . . . you can remain safe.
- *Direction is important . . . to where your work takes you.* Be aware of the unusual work areas or work duties you may be assigned to. Keep an eye out for lurking dangers.
- *Decisions are a dominant part of your workday.* An *unwise* decision can lead to an *unsafe* act. Seek to make decisions based on common sense and sufficient information. Get all the facts you need.

- *Deception can be the consequence of your own reasoning "fooling" you.* Don't try to *figure out* if something is safe. Rather, *find out* if it is safe . . . by inquiring after someone who will know.
- *Determination can throw caution to the wind.* You have to always keep at the forefront of your mind that your primary goal is to keep safe, not to get the job done.
- *Dissatisfaction can cause you to become careless with your work.* Even if you're dissatisfied with your work, you're still required to work safe. Be responsible . . . whether the work is pleasant or unpleasant.
- *Distinction is critical to avoid getting things mixed up or mistaking things for other things.* Organization is key. Management is a must. Keep it simple. Keep everything updated and properly tagged or labeled.
- *Destruction can be the current condition of a work area.* If you're required to work in such a work area, avoid danger spots. Keep a safe distance from operating equipment in use in dealing with the particularly ruined part of that work area.
- *Devotion should not be allowed to hold you in a dangerous area of the workplace.* Because the company can count on you to be in a certain work area each and every workday doesn't mean you have to be there when it is unsafe to be there.
- *Demoralization can be the result of superiors or super-mad coworkers grilling you . . . about something you either did or did not do.* This can cause you to drop your mental guard and drift through the workday . . . unaware of what all is going on around you.
- *Dysfunction can happen in a work environment where you feel "under attack" by fellow workers, who may do things "on the sly," to you.* Report it. Don't try to get through the workday with it. You may not be strong enough of heart to withstand it.

Even Good Workers Are Guilty!

● Safety truth:

All employees have . . . in some way or another . . . **committed** *safety violation, and have* **come short of** *the company's perfect standard of a safe workplace.*

If this is true, then even good workers are guilty . . . of safety violation. At some time or another, they have "cut corners" or have taken shortcuts.

Good workers are not *perfect*.

They're subject to temptation as any other employee on the job . . . and they sometimes yield.

Whether their safety violation is *exposed* or *excused*, their good work ethics remain unaffected . . . and not unappreciated.

Good workers may commit safety violation for a number of reasons, of which some are:

- Impatience—the hurrying factor
- Fatigue—the weakening factor
- Overconfidence—the self-motivating factor
- Pride—the determining factor

Because they *mean well* doesn't necessarily mean they will *make wise decisions*.

Decisions decide acts.

An unwise decision is a seed for an unsafe act.

An unsafe act is an *invitation* to an *incident*.

An incident can be an event (or something that happens) brought about by one's decision-based act.

↳ ***Acts*** *can create* **actual events!**

Good workers must make it their personal quest to be *responsible* workers.

Responsible workers own their responsibility to be safe.

To be safe is not a *request* but a *responsibility*.

A responsibility will be fulfilled by a *mature person*.

A mature person is the first stage to being a safe worker.

↳ *Where there is no* **maturity** *there will be* **mischief!** *Count on it!*

A steel mill is a *workplace* . . . not a *kindergarten*.
- ▶ A workplace is for *mature adults*.
- ▶ A kindergarten is for *mere kids*.

Childish people *play on the job* . . . as their usual activity.
Playing on the job can cause a serious matter.
A serious matter can be an injury or a fatality.
A fatality is the ultimate price for playing on the job.

A Mega P.Y.T.H.O.N. Moves in the Workplace!

● Safety truth:

> *Discipline in the form of **action** and **admonition** helps the safety violator to learn to not violate safety rules; but a safety violator who goes undisciplined disgraces the company.*

There is what I call a mega P.Y.T.H.O.N. that moves in the workplace. Using the word *PYTHON* as an acronym, I let each letter stand for the following:

Practice
You
Tend (to)
Have (that)
Overdrives
Non-compliance

There is a mega practice you . . . as an employee . . . tend to have that overdrives non-compliance with safety rules. I refer to it as a mega practice for the really simple fact that it has "preyed on" virtually every employee in the workplace. It is not necessarily a practice of committing the *same* safety violation, but committing safety violation in general that may entail doing different unsafe things.

This mega P.Y.T.H.O.N. is a real "predator" in the workplace, which seizes and squeezes the "life" out of a zealous company's safety efforts. At some point, an employee will entertain the idea of committing a safety violation . . . at a seemingly *ideal time* . . . when no one else is around or isn't looking. A practice of committing safety violation you tend to have overdrives your non-compliance. It pushes you to refuse to comply with company safety rules and to ignore safety warnings, as given by the company, at times.

Safety is a *challenge* that's posed to the workplace.
The workplace has to trust in its *champion.* The general manager is the workplace's safety champion.
For this very reason, the safety champion will also have to take on the P.Y.T.H.O.N.
The P.Y.T.H.O.N. "preys on" unsuspecting workers.
▶ The *world* is its natural "habitat."
▶ The *workplace* is its favorite "hunting ground."
The P.Y.T.H.O.N. is a "constrictor."
It "constricts" or squeezes safety practices "to death."
It feeds off of workers' foolishness in the workplace. Their foolish practices help keep it alive and well.

Don't Drink W.I.N.E. Lest You Forget the Safety Rules!

● Safety truth:

> *If an employee should **normalize** unsafe ways which he partakes of and becomes intoxicated with, he will **neglect** the safety rules.*

There are *safe* ways of doing your job.
There are *unsafe* ways of doing your job.
Ways you practice you will practically adopt.
Ways you practice you discipline yourself to walk in.
Ways you *discipline* yourself to walk in you *develop* as **habits.**
Habits are normal to you. They are the norm for you.

Using the word *WINE* as an acronym, I let each letter stand for the following:

Ways (that)
Intoxicate
Neglectful
Employees

The truth of the matter is that unsafe ways you practice will eventually "intoxicate" you. They will "poison" your safe practices and safe performance in the workplace.

Unsafe ways you learn as habits will cause you to neglect the safety rules.

"Drunk" as a Skunk!

The worker who has unsafe habits is what I call "drunk" as a skunk!

He's so full of his unsafe practices that he disregards the safety rules with foolish boldness and reckless overconfidence.

If you *disregard* the safety rules, they won't *do* you any good. For this very reason, you should:

1. *Trust in* the safety rules as the "shields" they're designed to be for you. If you're not shielded, then you're exposed to the possibility of being harmed.
2. *Try* to be safe by honoring the safety rules. The safety rules you won't keep, cannot keep you safe.
3. *Treasure* your body parts and your very life. Regard them as being of far greater importance to you than getting the job at hand done. What is irreplaceable is priceless.
4. *Trim* the "fat" of your foolishness, to reveal the "leanness" of a safety law-abiding employee in the workplace.
5. *Triumph over* every temptation to take the unsafe way . . . of doing things. Every such temptation you resist is a dangerous path you refuse to walk on.
6. *Transform* yourself from being an unsafe worker to becoming a safe worker by making a quality decision to be safe and to be a constant reminder to them that work with you that safety is number one. Others are *looking at* you . . . and some of whom are *learning* your ways of doing things.

Your ways of performing your work from day to day in the workplace are very important because of how they can *affect* your own safety.

Consider this personal questionnaire:

- Of *whom?*
- Of *what?*
- Of *when?*
- Of *where?*
- Of *why?*
- Of *how?*
- Of *to what extent or degree?*

Take in every possible, conceivable thing. Leave no stone unturned. Safety is just that important! Ask questions.
- ▶ Questions can reveal what has been overlooked.
- ▶ Questions can expose flaws in your most carefully laid plans to get your job done.
- ▶ Questions can spark a necessary quest for *more information.*

Don't underestimate the value of questions!

Questions cause you to consider things from a different perspective.

A different perspective is sometimes needed.

A different perspective can cause you to see your ways of doing your work in a new light . . . and with new insight and fresh understanding.

Question what you consider doing . . . before you do it!

Questions are your friends . . . not your enemies!

Questions aren't a waste of time . . . and more specifically, your time!

Welcome them!

Value them!

My Wish List for the Workplace

● Safety truth:

*If **safety** is greater than **success** to you, then you will gladly bear the burden of your unfinished work rather than to sorrowfully bear the burden of the consequence of your unsafe act.*

Personally, I have a wish list for the workplace.

The workplace is occupied by or filled with precious human beings.

Precious human beings have to learn to take their own safety seriously, and to take the necessary steps to be safe.

Here is my wish list for the workplace:

- I wish every worker would not only *attend* safety meetings but also *attain to* understanding of what is said and seriously presented to them.
- I wish every worker would not only *perform* his work safely but also *perceive* the crucial importance of doing so.
- I wish every worker would not only embrace the *vision* of a safe workplace but also realize that they themselves are the *vehicles* that will take the company to the glorious realization thereof.
- I wish every worker would not only believe there are *answers* to safety problems but also there are *actions* they must take in seeing the solutions to those safety problems.
- I wish every worker would not only *favor* the righteous cause of safety but also *find* acceptable ways and means of winning their safety cause.
- I wish every worker would not only have *clear* vision but also a genuine willingness to deal with a *cluttered* mind.
- I wish every worker would not only *choose* to do the right thing but also *change* his way of doing things, if it is unsafe.
- I wish every worker would not only see the "disease" of desperation as *curable* but also see that every unsafe condition is *conquerable*.
- I wish every worker would not only perceive *work* as being a chief necessity of life but also *wisdom*.
- I wish every worker would not only *set* safety as his personal goal but also *see* it as a definite must.
- I wish every worker would not only *break* unsafe habits but also *bring* awareness of safety concerns to others.
- I wish every worker would not only *consider* his way of doing things but also *connect with* coworkers who have ingenuous practical ways of performing their work safely.
- I wish every worker would not only *hear* the instruction to be safe but also *heed* it.
- I wish every worker would not only be *innocent* of safety violation but also be *involved* in the noble effort to greatly minimize safety violation.

- I wish every worker would not only be *quiet* to hear about others' incidents but also be *quick* to change their minds about how they carry out their work duties, when they're in conflict with safety.
- I wish every worker would not only forbear to judge *people* but also to be wise to judge *practices*.
- I wish every worker would not only *learn* to be safe but also *love* to teach others to be safe.

Every worker who cares about his or her coworker should care about safety and therefore should have their own wish list for the place they work at and report to daily.

A wish list may seem *primitive* but it is a *perfect* start to position yourself to have a personally safe work shift, as you enter the workplace daily or on your scheduled workdays.

Remember, if you're not being a part of the *safety solution*, then you're being a part of the *safety problem*.

Workplace safety depends on each individual worker . . . being committed to do the right thing in each instance.

Consider sitting down to write down *your own* wish list for your workplace. It just may open your eyes to new possibilities of safety practices and safety principles. You may actually *realize* something others failed to consider or see!

Seeing it on paper can give you a clearer picture of what you hope to see achieved in the workplace, in terms of having a safe place to work.

Owning a "Field" of Workers

● Safety truth:

*Any **unsafe** action is an **unquestionable** risk of jeopardizing the safety goal.*

The workplace, as it were, is a "field" that is owned by the company.

The company must consider the kinds of "seeds" it plants in its "field."

The company must give careful thought to the kinds of people it hires into its workplace.

▶ A *good seed* is a safe person.
▶ A *bad seed* is an unsafe person.

The interesting problem with this is that when the company hires a person, it doesn't know what *kind of* person it's really getting. That's why persons the company may consider hiring may be *asked about*.

The company must not only look for persons who're good at being *productive*.

It must also look for persons who're good at being *practically safe*.

The basic key to the "harvest" of a safe workplace is to plant "seeds" of safe persons in the workplace.

However, the company will only really know what it *has* when it *hires* people.

People have to be given the common opportunity and fair chance to prove what kind of workers they will be . . . in the workplace.

The real fact of the matter is that new hires are new risks for new incidents.

Incidents cannot only be *lived through;* they can also be *learned from*.

The company owns a "field" of workers.
Workers are famously known for using their hands.
Their hands are what get the brutally brunt of the work done.
But their *hands* aren't their only valuable assets.
Their *heads* house their minds.
Their minds are thinking machines.
Thinking machines should accompany *working machines*.
Working machines are operating equipment.

A "field" of workers should be "watered" with the wisdom of workplace safety.

If it is not, that "field" of workers will eventually "wither" or weaken in the purpose of safety.

It is perfectly understandable that a workplace can have both safe workers and unsafe workers. But a wise company will let the "tares" (unsafe workers) "grow up with" the "wheat" (safe workers), and then "weed out" every unsafe worker as they're convicted of safety violations and conclusively dealt with.

Three Basic Tools Every Worker Is Born With and Carries throughout His Life

● Safety truth:

> A **patient** worker is better than a **proud** worker. The patient one will listen and understand how to really be safe. The proud one will be self-confident, thinking that nothing will happen to him.

There are three basic tools that every worker is naturally born with and carries throughout his life . . . granted he doesn't lose any of them to personal injury.

They are:

1. Born with **hands.** Hands:
   - *Handle* the work.
   - *Hold* tools and other things.
   - *Help* others.

2. Born with **a head.** A head houses a *mind*. A mind:
   - *Processes* information.
   - *Produces* ideas.
   - *Prepares* strategies.

3. Born with **a heart.** A heart:
   - Has the capacity to *care*.
   - Has the concern to *caution others*.
   - Has the willingness to *communicate feelings*.

Be grateful for your natural tools. Cherish them. Respect them.
Your hands are *first-contacting tools.*
Your head is a *figuring tool.*
Your heart is a *feeling tool.*
When your hands are used in conjunction with your head and heart, they form an invisible key to unlock your personal safety!

3 Beautiful Keys to Being a Safe Worker

1. ***Doing* the right thing.** You have to *continually* choose to do the right thing. The right thing is the right path of performing your job to take. Don't depart from the right way of doing things.
   ▶ Expect ***distractions.*** Be determined to remain focused.
   ▶ Expect ***daily temptations.*** Be ready to resist them.

Safety is *war*.

In this regard, the workplace is a *war zone*.

You have to fight to keep safe. Safety is not an easy prize to claim. An incident is always waiting in the wings . . . ready to be introduced into your work shift.

2. ***Discovering* inner peace about doing the right thing.** If you don't have *peace* about what you're doing, then you have a *problem*. Unless that problem is resolved, you won't be able to work with confidence. Confidence makes working safe easier for you. Peace [inner peace] is a real proof of confidence. Confidence is a sweet product of knowing and understanding what to do.
3. ***Delighting* to do the right thing.** Just as you should take joy in teamwork, you should take joy in doing the right thing. Doing the right thing should make you *feel good* . . . and give you a wonderful sense of noble pride.

Workers who have a hard time delighting to do the right thing can be (a) desperate, (b) impatient, (c) proud, (d) angry, and (e) depressed.

Cardinal Rules: Seven "Deadly Sins"

● Safety truth:

*Safety must not only be your **talk**; it must also be your **walk**. That is how you can hope to make it [safe and sound] through your workday.*

There are five cardinal rules that steel mills universally recognize and have resolved within themselves to faithfully observe and to firmly enforce. They are:

- Lockout/Tagout/Tryout
- Fall Protection
- Confined Space
- Rail Safety
- Overhead Loads

Violation of a cardinal rule could result in your immediate *discharge* . . . or your immediate *death*.

They are five fiercely serious attempts of the company to keep you safe . . . and alive.

However, I want to delve into *deeper depths* of these noble cardinal rules, to see what new "treasure" of valuable insights I can come up with.

I "see" five very valuable insights from these five cardinal rules . . . plus two additional "jewels" of understanding.

Mathematically: 5 + 2 = 7.

Here is what I prefer to call seven "deadly sins" or very serious unsafe practices you should be totally aware of. Every employee, beyond the shadow of a doubt, should be in full possession of this potent foundational knowledge. It could very well save your life.

Your life is worth every highly zealous effort of the company, to save it.

7 "Deadly Sins": Some of the Most Dangerously Unsafe Practices in the Workplace

1. ***Locking out* your awareness of what's going on around you.**
   I glean this precious nugget of insight from the cardinal rule of Lockout/Tagout/Tryout. You can do this by:

   - *Daydreaming*—being in your own little "world"
   - *Distraction*—shifting your focus unnecessarily . . . and unwisely

- *Determination*—unwilling to accept defeat
- *Depression*—feeling like the whole world is weighing down on you

2. **Looking to do things that are over your head.** I glean this precious nugget of insight from the cardinal rule of Overhead Loads. Things that are over your head are *beyond your ability*. What is beyond your ability is *too much* for you to take on or handle. What you cannot *handle* can *hurt* you. You have to stay in the "lane" of your ability. If you don't, you risk having an "accident." Your *inability* to cope with a particular problem can cause you to have an *incident*. Think about it.
3. **Leaving your safety zone.** I glean this precious nugget of insight from the cardinal rule of Confined Space. Your safety zone is the area where you're safe from danger or dangerous conditions. One single step outside the safety zone immediately places you in the danger zone. The danger zone is any area where danger or dangerous conditions prevail. You should not be there . . . unless authorized to be there.
4. **Learning unsafe habits.** I glean this precious nugget of insight from the cardinal rule of Rail Safety. Unsafe habits can be learned by studying them practiced by fellow workers or experimented with in your own ways of doing your job. The word *invention* comes to mind. You can actually invent new ways and means of doing your work . . . which may be dangerous or totally unsafe. You can create a death trap for yourself. *How* you use your tools and operating equipment can transform them into instruments of death. Whatever way or means you *devise,* you must make sure it isn't *dangerous* . . . to you or anyone else.
5. **Leaping before you look.** I glean this precious nugget of insight from the cardinal rule of Fall Protection. This is roughly interpreted as *charging* headlong before *checking out:*
   ▶ The **action** you decide to *execute;* or,
   ▶ The **area** you decide to *enter.*

   Learn to send your eyes ahead of you, to "spy out the land" or check out the prevailing conditions which may lie before you.

   Before you *do* anything, *discuss* [with yourself or someone else] how you should do it and *determine* if you'll need any help to accomplish it.

Look before you leap . . . into action!

6. ***Listening to* dangerous counsel.** Dangerous counsel can come from daredevils on the job—those who take foolish risks with their own limbs . . . and lives. If an unsafe worker—who you well know is unsafe—gives you dangerous advice on what to do, you SHOULD NOT consent to it. You SHOULD KNOW BETTER than to follow any course of action that could prove to be *fatal* to you.
7. ***Losing* your respect for what can harm you.** If you lose your *respect* for it, you also lose your *real advantage* of recognizing and knowing what can harm you. Some operating equipment can be a "beast." If you *fail* to respect it, then it just might *feast on* you. The usual scenario of "predator and prey" will be played out . . . at your mistake and misfortune.

SAFETY COUNSEL FOR YOU TO CONSIDER

- Your *job* may not bring you *joy*, but don't let boredom supersede your focus. Your focus means everything . . . in the workplace.
- Your *doubt* about something can be a real warning of potential *danger*.
- No matter what's going on, *get informed* before you *get involved*.
- Always remember your *safety* is also for the *sake* of others.
- If there's uncertainty about anything, *ask* questions before you *act*.
- Whatever you *dare* to do you may *die* trying to do it! Sometimes, death is the result of trying to prove a point.
- Your *action* should be accompanied by *caution*. Caution should definitely mark the common worker.
- Use your *hearing* as well as your *head*. Learn to interpret the various noises made in your workplace.
- Don't try to *play hero*. Rather, *play it safe*. The company expects you to be a *safe worker* . . . not a *superhero*.
- What you do not *report* you let *remain* a trap . . . for someone else.
- *Animosity* in the workplace evidences *adversaries* among workers. This can seriously hinder reaching the safety goal.

5

Wearing S.T.E.E.L. Toe Boots: Walk in Wisdom!

● Safety truth:

> *The company can supply you with **safety equipment**, but it cannot supply you with **self-love**.*

Using the word *STEEL* as an acronym, I let each letter stand for the following:

Safety
Tips (and)
Employee
Empowerment
Lessons

As a worker in the workplace, you have to learn to walk in wisdom on safety.

Wisdom on safety is possessed by a wise worker.

A wise worker knows (or finds out) what's safe and what's unsafe.

A wise worker understands how to be safe and greatly respects what has real potential to harm him. He knows unsafe acts are choices that will produce consequences . . . which may not be favorable for him. He knows and appreciates the real value of his very life. *He doesn't want to get hurt . . . or killed!* So he chooses to be wise about his conduct and continuing performance in the workplace.

The workplace can potentially be the place of his death.

How you *walk* [or conduct yourself] in the workplace is just as important as how you *work* in the workplace.

You can be unsafe:

- When going to break
- When going the way where heavy equipment is well-known to be found
- When going to the cafeteria . . . to get something to eat
- When going to the restroom . . . not watching while walking towards it
- When going to areas unauthorized to you
- When going into "play mode" . . . to engage in horseplay on the job
- When going into your "own world" . . . or daydreaming

Here are some safety tips, to empower you to walk in safety wisdom, to help keep you safe. However, you have to *respect* them; otherwise, they won't do you any good.

7 Safety Tips On: Going to Break

1. **Keep on the PPE required until you've cleared that particular area and have entered an area where it's safe to remove it.** An incident can happen within the timeframe of *exiting the work area* to *entering the break area*.
2. **Keep your head on the swivel. Watch for oncoming danger, such as approaching motorized vehicles.** Break time isn't necessarily time to let your guard down. An incident is as a *predator* . . . that's always on the hunt for a "prey." Don't position yourself to become a "prey."
3. **Keep clear of sharp objects (that can cut you), trip hazards, immediate areas where work is under way, stacks that can potentially fall, etc.** There are always things to look out for.

Always. Just as if you *stop* breathing you will die, if you *stop* being safe you will get hurt.
4. **Keep your mind on where you're at and be aware of your immediate surroundings.** A *safe* worker is a *seeing* worker. He sees all he can possibly see. He doesn't turn a blind eye to anything. He *inspects* his work environment.
5. **Keep an eye out for unsafe conditions, unsafe equipment, and unsafe workers.** *Unnoticed* things can be *unsafe* things. Unsafe things need to be corrected . . . immediately.
6. **Keep to a safe pathway to where you want to go.** Be wisely selective of the way you choose to take, considering what's found along the way. Don't be *ambushed* by an incident.
7. **Keep the safety practice of turning off your operating equipment and putting your tools somewhere they won't be trip hazards . . . for you or others.** Responsibility shouldn't be given a break. It should be working continually. To give it *time off* is to give an incident a *chance to happen*.

7 Safety Tips On: Going in the Way of Heavy Equipment

1. **Respect its right of way . . . at all times.** Your physical body is *very fragile*. Respect that natural fact. It cannot possibly withstand the awesomely brutal force of heavy equipment. Heavy equipment is very quite capable of exerting tremendous crushing force.
2. **Respect its dangerous potential . . . to harm you.** It may be designed to serve you, but understand it is also designed to serve a specific function. It will do what it's designed to do . . . even if you *happen* to get in its way. It won't stop for you . . . of its own accord. Compassion cannot be built into it. Respect that . . . continually.
3. **Respect its sounded warnings . . . by way of its horn being blown at you.** It is a sound for life . . . not death. It is a sound to *preserve* you. Don't ignore its warning sounds.
4. **Respect its regular routes . . . in the workplace.** Don't deliberately venture into dangerous territory, especially when you

know better. It can result in your workday being the day of your death.
5. **Respect its load or line of work.** That only makes it *even more* dangerous. It increases its crushing force. More weight means more crushing power.
6. **Respect its lack of human capacity for your concern.** It doesn't *feel.* It only does what it is made/designed to do.
7. **Respect its "blind spots" . . . for that its operator may not see you . . . in time.** Always make yourself *visible.* Don't be a *hidden object.* A hidden object is subject to being hurt . . . or destroyed.

7 Safety Tips On: Going to the Cafeteria

1. **Don't let your hunger become your huge distraction.** Hunger can *weaken* your focus on what you need to be focused. That's why you should eat a *sufficient* amount of food, to tide you over until it is break time. Break time is time you can safely eat.
2. **Don't think *food.* Think *focus!*** A growling stomach and a moving force of equipment don't really create a favorable scenario. To be hungry is not a good way to be safe. Your mind must be kept in *expecting* mode . . . not *eating* mode. Expect the unexpected.
3. **Don't *count* your money while walking . . . and being "blind" to what's going on around you.** *Don't let your dollars distract you.* You can count your money when you arrive safely at the cafeteria.
4. **Don't let a sudden conversation claim your undivided attention. Pay attention to where you're going and who or what is coming your way.** If you don't *pay attention* to what can harm you, an incident just may *pay you a visit.*
5. **Don't take forbidden or dangerous routes.** Safety has its safe paths . . . to take. But to take them, you must *know* them. You must *discern* the difference between a safe route and an unsafe route.
6. **Don't try to "outrun" moving cranes or moving vehicles in the vicinity.** You may risk running to your own death. Patience is a powerful weapon, to ward off incidents. Either be *patient* or *perish.*

7. **Don't engage in horseplay while on the way to the cafeteria.** An incident is always *potentially hidden* in horseplay. You may not make it to the cafeteria. You may make it to the hospital . . . or the morgue.

7 Safety Tips On: *Going to the Restroom*

1. **Be attentive. Hold your head up . . . not down. Pay attention to where you're going and what's coming towards you.** An incident is not *limited to location*. It is subject to happen practically anywhere . . . in the workplace. The workplace has restrooms. Restrooms are no real guarantee that nothing will happen.
2. **Be mindful of flying objects that are subject to suddenly go airborne.** The sound of crashing should not be ignored. You should immediately look around, to see if any thing is flying through the air, and prepare to duck and dodge it, if you can. *Sounds can be safety warnings.*
3. **Be responsible to not pull out your cell phone while on the way to the restroom.** A cell phone is a distraction you can carry with you. A distraction you can carry with you can always be a *common cause* of an incident.
4. **Be cautious of the route you take to the restroom.** Avoid dangerous areas, where work is under way. In this regard, the workplace is as a "minefield." Beware of the hidden "mines" or unsafe conditions that are really there. Don't go the way where they are at. *Choose an alternate route* . . . one that will get you safely to the restroom.
5. **Be certain that people operating moving equipment are aware of you . . . and where you're at.** Communicate with them. Get their attention. *Make sure they see you!* Don't *assume* they see you. They may not!
6. **Be careful while in the restroom. It's no place to let your safety guard down.** Beware of slippery surfaces, trip hazards, electrical dangers, spiders, etc. The restroom may be a place where you can safely relax . . . for a moment . . . but not to relax your vigilance. An incident can happen *in a moment.*

7. **Be minded to put proper PPE back on before leaving the restroom . . . if it leads directly back onto the work floor.** *Check before you charge out the door!* Make sure you have on your hard hat and safety glasses, especially.

7 Safety Tips On: Going to Unauthorized Areas

1. **Let your supervisor/superior know where you're going.** Don't go on *"secret missions."* Make sure you have on the proper PPE for entering . . . and remaining . . . in those unauthorized areas.
2. **Let the people, who work in those particular areas, know of your presence there.** Don't be an *unknown element* there. *Make yourself known!* Wave at them, to indicate your presence there. Holler at them, if you have to. Do what's necessary . . . and safe . . . to get their attention, to alert them of your presence.
3. **Let the heavy operating equipment there have the right of way.** Your well-being and very life depend on it. A car crossing the railroad tracks is no match for a speeding train. Remember: You're that "car." That heavy operating equipment is that "speeding train." Don't foolishly risk it! In the end, it won't be worth it.
4. **Let the dangerous conditions of those areas be continually respected by you.** Question: If you recognized a poisonous snake, would you try to play with it? Likewise, don't make light of dangerous conditions. Respect them . . . for the *real harm* they pose to you.
5. **Let your rigid adherence to safety rules guide you in those areas.** Safety rules are not to just *know.* They are to *never be violated.*
6. **Let your lack of safety training in those areas be a constant reminder to not get the "big head" to bravely explore those dangerous areas . . . alone.** Don't try to *go* where you don't have a *guide* . . . to accompany you. Be careful about taking your own tours of the workplace. Know the safe routes and safe spots. Know what's off limits to you and respect them.
7. **Let the tools and equipment practically used in those areas, which you're unfamiliar with, alone.** Just as it's dangerous for

a child to handle a loaded gun, it's dangerous for you to handle tools and equipment which you don't have good understanding of and haven't been properly trained in their correct and safe use. *Don't be a child in the workplace!* The workplace is no place for a child to be . . . to aimlessly wander.

7 Safety Tips On: Going into "Play Mode"

1. **Do not play with someone while they're working.** I'm not referring to horseplay, which is rough play; rather, I'm talking about "light fun." You can cause them to get hurt . . . to lose a body part or their life. *Pick your playful times.* Don't do any thing to endanger yourself or others. A safe worker knows when it's safe to play . . . with a fellow worker.
2. **Do not play with tools and equipment you don't understand or know how to properly use.** If a child plays with matches, he may get burned. If you mess with things you don't really understand, you may get "burned" for doing so. It can be a very painful experience. *Be safe or burn.*
3. **Do not play in dangerous areas.** Dangerous areas are places with ideal conditions perfect for "breeding" incidents. As fishes in ponds waiting to be *caught,* incidents in dangerous areas are waiting to be *caused.*
4. **Do not play with dangerous chemicals.** Dangerous chemicals can harm you. You can incur life-time regrets for doing so. A disfigured body part, a missing eye (that was burned out), a breathing problem—these are just a few of life-time regrets you could end up with.
5. **Do not play with your life or other people's lives.** Don't make light of what is priceless or impossible for you to replace. Human life has *far greater value* than anything else in the workplace.
6. **Do not play by hitching a ride on moving equipment . . . whether on the ground or in the air.** *You are asking for it.* You are being unsafe. You are being irresponsible. You are being a terrible example to them watching you. You are grievously disappointing the company. You are showing lack of genuine concern for your own well-being.

7. **Do not play with people in other work areas, only to distract them . . . from their work and their being safe.** *Speak* to them, but don't *spook* them! Don't mess with them while they may be messing with tools and equipment. Don't bother them while they're handling things. They need their focus. Their very work requires their undivided attention. Be safe . . . and help to keep them safe . . . by not distracting them.

7 Safety Tips On: Going into Your "Own World"

1. **Know that going into your "own world" is daydreaming.** Daydreaming makes you a "sitting duck" for an incident. An incident has no respect of persons.
2. **Know that daydreaming is a dangerous distraction.** A dangerous distraction can cause you to pay a terrible price. A terrible price can be one of your limbs or even your life.
3. **Know that daydreaming renders you totally unaware of your immediate surroundings.** Your immediate surroundings can contain real dangers. Real dangers can come "knocking at your door," while you're in your own world.
4. **Know that daydreaming makes you very vulnerable . . . to what can hurt or kill you.** A safe worker protects himself by staying alert. Staying alert is key to staying alive.
5. **Know that daydreaming makes you an easy target for an incident.** An incident will come upon you like a thief in the night. You have to be vigilant. Your eyes can be open and your mind *somewhere else*. Keep your mind in the exact location of where you are.
6. **Know that daydreaming makes you an unreliable worker.** An unreliable worker isn't responsible to remain focused . . . on the tasks assigned to him. He would rather be *somewhere else* . . . other than the workplace.
7. **Know that daydreaming will make you incident-prone.** Daydreaming makes you a danger to others. It cripples your critical focus. It renders you *out of touch with reality* for the length of time you're in your "own world." Anything is subject to happen while you're not "at home."

Walking by Faith . . . To Reach the Safety Goal

● Safety truth:

> *If you **trust** something you haven't **tried out** yet, it might fail you . . . right when you need it most . . . to work for you.*

Let me let you in on a little secret: It is impossible to reach the safety goal without *faith*.

Faith is confidence.

Confidence can be put in a person . . . or thing.

▶ You can have confidence in *God*.
▶ You can have confidence in *other people*.
▶ You can have confidence in *yourself*.

All the employees of the workplace *must believe* they can reach the safety goal.

To reach the safety goal, they *must believe* they can be safe.

☞ *What you don't believe you **can be**, you **won't be**!*

10 Big Keys to Believe You Can Be Safe

1. **You can be safe because it is a *personal choice*.** You can choose to be safe or unsafe.
2. **You can be safe because it is a *possible feat*.** It can be done. Because it can be done, you can do it!
3. **You can be safe because of the company's *practical efforts* to make the workplace safe.** The company diligently strives to improve its workplace safety-wise. This is quite evident by the company's work of installing guards wherever it can, buying all types of gloves for its employees to work with, adding or subtracting whatever needs to be, for safety's sake, etc.
4. **You can be safe because of your *past performance* of being safe.** You've done it before. You can do it again!

5. **You can be safe because of the *passionate concern* of coworkers.** Coworkers are also *protectors* for you . . . in a real sense . . . as they help to watch out for you.
6. **You can be safe because of the *protective equipment* you're furnished with.** The company is willing to replace what you may accidentally lose or simply wear out. Why? Because the company wants you to be safe! It does its part . . . in helping keep you safe.
7. **You can be safe because of *prudent decisions* you can make.** Your actions are the products of your decisions. Your decisions decide your *fortunate outcomes* or your *fate*.
8. **You can be safe because of your *permanent respect* for what can harm you.** If it can harm you, respect it! It's just that outrageously simple!
9. **You can be safe because the *production goal* is outweighed by the safety goal.** The company would rather lose out on production . . . and prospective customers . . . than lose lives in its workplace.
10. **You can be safe because your *proud family* can be a dependable source of inspiration for you.** You matter to them. To them, you're a precious jewel they don't wish to lose. They know they could lose you to a job accident.

A Y.E.L.L.O.W. Hat: What Young Workers Should Want . . . And Wisely Pursue

● Safety truth:

> *A good worker will use* **strength** *but a safe worker will use* ***strategy.***

There's a key observation I've made in the workplace over the years. It mainly concerns young men and old men.

Young men tend to be childish. They're prone to play a lot. They can even be too proud to listen . . . especially to older hands.

Older hands to whom I refer are old men.

Old men tend to be mature. They take life seriously. They've learned the real value of being good listeners.

Good listeners make good learners.
Good learners make good workers.
Good workers are what the company wants . . . and hopes to have, as they hire and hand out *yellow hats*.

Using the word *YELLOW* as an acronym, I let each letter stand for the following:

Young
Employees
Listening to (and)
Learning from
Older
Workers

Proverbs 20:29 states:

> *The glory of young men is their strength: and the beauty of old men is the grey head.*

Let me put my thoughts here in perspective.

● Young men have *youth*.

Youth gifts them with *strength*.
Strength is the state or quality of being *strong*.
The company (I've referring to steel mills) wants strong workers because of the demanding hands-on work which is required to be done.
Young men are ideal workers for this kind of work.
Young men, characteristically, are:

- *Physically* strong
- *Wonderfully* able-bodied
- *Naturally* energetic
- *Joyfully* have good stamina

Young men may have the *muscles* to do the hard work, but they must also have the *mind* to work smart . . . and safe. They tend to "show off" their strength . . . much like bodybuilders who "show off" their physiques on stage before many people . . . and love doing it.

- ● Old men have *grey heads*.

Grey heads are generally accepted signs of *wisdom*.
Wisdom isn't innate. They weren't born with it. They *attained* it over the course of their lives.
Old men are seen as wise men.
As wise men, they've lived through much, witnessed much, and studied much . . . in the workplace.
The workplace has been their *school of learning* . . . over their working years. As a wonderful consequence, they've become *beautifully wise*.
Old men, characteristically, are:

- *Apt* to teach
- *Able* to train
- *Aware* of potential dangers
- *Attentive* to trainees' needs and concerns

Old men may have *declined* in physical strength, but they make up for that in that they have *discovered* a wealth of workplace wisdom . . . through their years of working on the job.

If young employees are smart, they'll learn to humble themselves under these "mighty hands" of older workers, who can help them to be successful and to rise in the ranks, in the workplace.
Young workers should allow older workers to:

- *Mentor* them.
- *Make* them wise workers.
- *Motivate* them.
- *Move* them in the right direction . . . and the safe way of doing things in the workplace.

But it causes for true humility of young workers and true concern of old workers. Old workers, who started out on the job as young workers, should be regarded as *teachers* by young workers. Young workers should regard themselves as *students* to older hands.

Note: I'm referring to old workers who *started out on the job as young workers, and grew old in that workplace.*

Walking in the Workplace As "Obedient Children"

● Safety truth:

*Safety is not a **request**. It is a **responsibility**.*

Interesting to me to note is a Scriptural passage found in Matthew 11:19, which states:

But wisdom is justified of her children.

As I pondered on this Scriptural passage, I began to perceive precious principles of workplace safety:

1. Wisdom on workplace safety is as a *mother* to workers in the workplace.
2. Workers in the workplace are as *children* to the "mother" of wisdom on workplace safety.

Workers should walk in the workplace as "obedient children."

As "obedient children," they should obey the *instructions* of their "mother" called wisdom on workplace safety.

When they hear and heed her instructions on safety, they will *observe* her prescribed ways of working safe.

When they observe her prescribed ways of working safe, they will be *happy and fortunate* for doing so.

- As "obedient children," they are *submissive* workers.
- As "obedient children," they are *safe* workers.

Safe workers obey safety instructions.

And, the converse is also true. Workers who won't obey safety instructions are as "disobedient children."

As "disobedient children," they don't keep the safety rules . . . consistently . . . as they should.

Consequentially, "disobedient children" will *expose* themselves to the very dangers their "mother" sought to protect them from.

▶ *Disobedient workers **endanger** themselves.*
▶ *Obedient workers **ensure** their personal safety.*

Where there is no *obedience* to safety instruction and safety rules there will be *opportunities* for incidents to happen.

Therefore:

☞ Obedience *minimizes* opportunities for incidents to happen.
☞ Disobedience *maximizes* opportunities for incidents to happen.

And therefore, the "mother" of wisdom on workplace safety is justified of her "children."

Her "children" will be either "obedient children," to obey her safety instructions and therefore will be happy and fortune for it; or, they will be "disobedient children," to disobey her safety instructions and therefore will suffer for it.

It's that simple.

5 Interesting Things That Safety Is

1. **Safety is a CHALLENGE.** Every workplace is posed with this challenge. However, the real question is: Are they up to the challenge? Unless this challenge is *answered*, the safety goal won't be *attained*. The workplace needs its *workers* . . . and the safety goal needs its *warriors*.
2. **Safety is a CHAMPIONSHIP.** Every workplace should want to have the position of a winner. Safety is a championship that any and every workplace can win. But the secret of victory lies within the solemn fact that each employee must do his or her part . . . of being safe. Being safe depends heavily on working smart.
3. **Safety is a CHAIN.** A chain is comprised of links. Each employee is a "link" in the "chain" of safety, in their workplace. An unsafe

employee is a *weak link*. As a weak link, that person will *hinder* the team effort to obtain the safety goal. When all employees are safe, they will be *strong links*. As strong links, the safety goal becomes easy to realize.
4. **Safety is a CHANGE.** It is a change *for the better*. It is a change for a *better place to work*. A change can be a key to *improvement*. An improved workplace is a *changed* workplace. A changed workplace begins with each employee changing himself, to unlearn unsafe habits and to adopt safe practices that will hopefully become safe habits.
5. **Safety is a CHOICE.** Each employee must choose to be safe . . . each and every workday . . . throughout the work shift. They must beware of whom or what they allow to *influence* their decisions . . . whether to be safe or to be unsafe. *The **choices** they make will create the **consequences** they experience.*

4 Common Things That Can Cause You Harm

1. **Your *pride*.** Your pride won't let you listen to instruction. You may *hear* it but you won't *heed* it. Instead, you will disdain it. As a proud worker, you *feel* that you don't need instruction because you consider yourself *self-sufficient at being safe*. But the frightening fact of the matter is that you can be harmed *for lack of specific information*. Specific information is conveyed by instruction. You need to humbly accept the real fact that you *don't know everything*. A humble worker always leaves room to *learn more*.
2. **Your *arrogance*.** Your arrogance is evidence of a superego. A superego makes you think more highly of yourself than you ought to think. It makes you think that you're a *dominant* worker. A dominant worker can sometimes be a *daredevil*. A daredevil will attempt to "show out" before others . . . to "show off" what you can skillfully do, in the workplace. A daredevil can *open a door* to his own demise.
3. **Your unsafe *way* . . . of doing things.** Your unsafe way is a key to unlock an incident. An incident can be a property damage, an injury, or a fatality. Your *unsafe* way will eventually lead to an

unexpected event. It's just a matter of time. Your dependence upon luck will prove foolish, as your luck will ultimately "run out." *Luck is an unreliable thing to rely on.*

4. **Your *perverse mouth*.** Your perverse mouth will speak things that are directed away from the right way and the safe way of doing things. You can give other employees *erroneous* instruction, which will lead them astray . . . from the right and safe way of performing their work. You can actually teach them shortcuts, as you seek to show them a "more excellent way" of doing their jobs. In so doing, you place their feet upon paths of destruction. You lead them into ways that are not good.

A Four-Star "General" . . . Leading An "Army" of Safe Workers

● Safety truth:

*Employees who hate **divine wisdom** of workplace safety love **death**.*

I see the general manager as a "general."
A general leads his army.
Similarly, I see the "general" (general manager) leading his "army" of safe workers in the workplace.
As a four-star "general," he has four "stars" or *superior qualities* which wisdom on workplace safety gives him.

✪ The superior quality of *sound counsel*. Counsel is advice or guidance. This "general" is well able to *guide* his "army" . . . of safe workers. As their guide, he:

- Supervises their education and training.
- Exerts influence over them.
- Steers them in the right . . . and safe . . . direction.

The safe workers will follow him with a sense of pride and noble courage. After all, he is their *safety champion*.

- ✪ The superior quality of *sound wisdom*. Wisdom is prudence. Prudence is caution in practical affairs. It is discretion or circumspection. This "general" leads an "army" of discreet workers . . . of circumspect persons . . . who're heedful of circumstances and potential consequences.
- ✪ The superior quality of *sound understanding*. Understanding is know-how or comprehension of the true nature of something. You can *know* what a tool or piece of equipment is, but do you *know how* to use it or operate it . . . properly and safely? This "general" leads an "army" of know-how workers, who know how to get the job done—and that in a safe manner.
- ✪ The superior quality of *sound strength*. Strength is the ability to maintain a moral or intellectual position firmly. This "general" leads an "army" of strong workers, who're strong in the sense that they maintain their moral position on being safe in the workplace. You simply cannot get them to change their position. They will fight to their last breath and die holding their position.

Where there is *wisdom* there will be *wise leadership*.

Wise leadership is a principal key to a successfully safe workplace. The leader of a workplace is the general manager.

The general manager is the "general" of an "army" of workers.

Wisdom on workplace safety is his "joint chief of staff" that advises him on safety matters.

Safety Rulership: A Four-Part Ranking System in the Workplace

- ● Safety truth:

    *All instructions in safety are **right** to employees who're discerning and are faultless to them that **really** know better.*

Working at a steel mill, I've observed that there is what I call a *safety rulership* in place.

This safety rulership is the position of *rulers* in the workplace.

Rulers in the workplace are those that hold the highest positions. Regarding safety rulership, I refer to them by royal titles. Why? Because royal persons are rulers.

I describe them in the following four-part ranking system below:

- *Safety kings.* They *reign* or exercise sovereign power in the workplace. They are general managers of the workplace. They want their workplace to be a *safe kingdom.*
- *Safety princes.* They *decree justice* and they *rule* . . . under the general manager. They are the assistant general manager, superintendents, and general foremen, of the workplace.
- *Safety nobles.* They're of noble rank or status. They are the safety directors, assistant safety directors, and the like, of the workplace.
- *Safety judges.* They are the supervisors, who *judge* or govern their crews, in the workplace. They rule, as well, as what they say goes, and any worker under them who refuses to do what they say, will be charged with insubordination. Insubordination can result in termination.

For a workplace to be safe, it must have *law and order.*

Law and order are what a safety rulership is ideally expected to bring to the workplace.

They're not "ruling" for *power* but for *performance.*

If they cannot get the job done, then a safe workplace cannot be achieved.

If a safe workplace cannot be achieved under their "safety rulership," then their "safety rulership" will be a failure.

A failure . . . of this magnitude . . . can mean final days of a workplace . . . and of their safety rule.

The C.L.O.C.K. Is Ticking!

● Safety truth:

> **Wisdom** *on workplace safety is better than* **wealth** *gained by bountiful profits . . . with injured or killed employees.*

Every workplace receives guidance and direction from its company.
I call this company's guidance and direction the C.L.O.C.K. Using the word *CLOCK* as an acronym, I let each letter stand for the following:

Company
Leadership
Of
Continual-improvement
Keys

Under company leadership, a workplace is ideally expected to prosper wonderfully by practical implementation of keys the company may wisely use, to continue improving the workplace and maintaining its good safety status.

Here are some *royal keys* which are purposefully designed to continually improve the workplace, to reach its safety goal and to retain the glorious status of "safe workplace":

10 Royal Keys to Continually Improve the Workplace

- **Wisdom** of workplace safety *cries out* in the workplace. The company should wisely be its voice, to continually proclaim its safety messages to its employees. These safety messages are commonly called *safety talks*.
- **Wisdom** of workplace safety should be *kept on top* . . . of everything else. It should always be the company's top priority . . . first place in order of importance . . . the company's main concern.
- **Wisdom** of workplace safety serves as the *gatekeeper* of the workplace. Before employees come through the entrance gate to enter the workplace, they should be safety-conscious.
- **Wisdom** of workplace safety *calls to* every worker in the workplace. Every worker in the workplace should attend safety meetings. Safety meetings should include safety talks.
- **Wisdom** of workplace safety mainly targets naïve employees—who don't understand how to be prudent—and foolish employees—who

lack an understanding heart. In fact, these are Safety's *problem workers*. They seem to have a problem with being safe.

- **Wisdom** of workplace safety gives excellent teaching and right direction. This is the basic key to building a workplace of wise employees. Wise employees are the *hopeful seeds* for safe employees.
- **Wisdom** of workplace safety presents *safety truths*. Safety truths always prove true . . . in every instance . . . in every workplace experience. There is no erroneous instruction; only right ways of doing things.
- **Wisdom** of workplace safety is for the ultimate benefit of the workers. The workers need a *vision* . . . of how to be safe. Without that vision, their hope of being a safe workplace will perish.
- **Wisdom** of workplace safety is introduced in a *simple way* . . . that even a child can grasp. There's nothing complex or complicated about it. It's plain and easy to understand to anyone with even half a mind!
- **Wisdom** of workplace safety must be *received* by the workers to whom it is given. Those that receive it will *retain* it . . . in their hearts and minds, to become a part of them. To bond with wisdom is, indeed, a beautiful thing.

■ These ten royal keys should be possessed and practically implemented by all steel mills that have a safety goal toward which they courageously and determinedly strive. Without the right keys, reached-for doors, found to be locked to them, cannot be opened.

Discovering the Secret of a Good Workday

● Safety truth:

*When you **follow** safety rules, they will **lead** you away from the "pits" of personal incidents.*

Incidents *pursue* safety violators.
Safety violators tend to have a bad workday.

A bad workday strongly suggests they need to discover the secret of a good workday.

The secret of a good workday lies within a good work shift.

A good work shift is dependent upon good performance.

Good performance is given by good workers.

Good workers must stay safe.

To stay safe, they must do the right things.

To do the right things, they have to resist temptation to do the wrong things.

To resist temptation to do the wrong things, they must be built up upon their most serious confidence.

Their most serious confidence should be that they *believe* they can be safe . . . throughout the entirety of their work shift.

Three excitingly inspiring words ring loud and clear in their hearts and minds:

JUST DO IT!

6 Keys to Discover the Secret of a Good Workday

1. **Be attentive.** Pay attention to what's going on . . . at all times. *Distraction can be disastrous . . . and deadly.*
2. **Be patient.** Don't get in a hurry. Safety is more important than saving time. Saving time is not as important as saving you.
3. **Be humble.** Pride can promise you a personal incident. Accept offered help from others. Consider their advice. Be willing to reconsider plans of action. Listen.
4. **Be cautious.** Take nothing you do for granted. Respect whatever may seem harmless . . . to be on the safe side. *Dangers can have all kinds of disguises.*
5. **Be appreciative . . . of friendly reminders and friendly suggestions.** A wise worker is open to suggestions of others. In fact, he expects them . . . from others. *A sea having rivers running into it always receives from them.* See fellow workers as "rivers" always "feeding" you friendly advice.
6. **Be your "brother's keeper."** Look out for your fellow worker, too. He's counting on you . . . to help keep him safe. The real truth that two are better than one should definitely mean

something to you. You may look out for yourself; but having someone else to also look out for you significantly increase your chances to be safe.

The Preaching Principle: Repent . . . To Realize a Really Safe Workplace

● Safety truth:

> The **first principle** to being a safe worker is to **faithfully respect** what can harm you.

If you can take the word "repent" that's found in the realm of the religious and innocently introduce it into the realm of real life, you can come up with what I call a *safety sermon*.

A safety sermon is simply a safety talk . . . purposefully designed to make you think about the way you do your job, and to convince you to change your mind about how you do your job . . . if it is unsafe.

Repent means to do a 180-degree turn in life. It means to stop going the wrong way and start going the right way.

Therefore, in regard to workplace safety, to *repent* is to change your mind about how you do things in the workplace. It means to stop going about the wrong way of doing things and start going about the right way of doing things.

In all probability, all workers are guilty of going about doing their jobs the wrong way . . . the unsafe way . . . especially when no one else is around or looking.

Particularly, these are the times when *shortcuts seem sweetest*.

But if you can *forgive* your "sins" or safety violations of the past, then you can move on to that next level . . . of being a boldly safe worker.

Though you may be remorseful, don't be too hard on yourself, to see yourself as a bad employee.

A bad employee is a bad image of you.

A bad image of you won't do much to encourage you.

You don't need *discouragement.* What you need is *determination* . . . to be a safe employee from thereon.

If you haven't been terminated for some safety violation, then you still have a *chance to change.*

You don't have to be a *perfect* employee to be a *safe* employee.

Perfection is unattainable in the human realm; but safety is well within your grasp. But you have to *want* it. It must bear *real significance* to you.

You cannot *procure* what you're unwilling to *pursue.*

Therefore, safety has to be a *personal pursuit.*

The workplace becomes genuinely . . . and wonderfully . . . safe, one employee being safe at a time.

Time in the workplace must be respected by the workers, who must have a *common vision* of it: To consider their time in the workplace as *time to be safe* . . . not as *time to get hurt.*

4 Identified Types of Individuals in the "World" of the Workplace

1. **"Wise men": Respectable workers.** These are the *"doers" in the workplace.* In doing the work, they are safe, quality-minded, and productive. Regarding safety, they know how to be safe. Regarding quality, they know what is acceptable and what is unacceptable. Regarding production, they come to work *to work!* They're determined to get the job done. They make a show of wisdom in their work performance and merit respect of the company. They're humble and good listeners, being the *ideal workers* that the company wishes all of its workers would be.
2. **"Wild beasts": Rebellious workers.** These are the *"difficult workers" in the workplace.* They're difficult to deal with. They insist on doing things their way. They really don't want to have to answer to someone else. They really don't like being told what to do. When they refuse to "bow down" to their superiors, the "seed" of their pride can produce for them the "harvest" of shame. They can be stubborn and overbearing. They will most likely be the ones that give supervisors the most trouble. Yet they can be

safe, quality-minded, and productive. It's their *attitude* . . . not their *ability* . . . that needs to be improved.

3. **"Wary fish": Recreant workers.** These are the *"dodgers" in the workplace*. They dodge work . . . as much as they possibly can . . . while trying to avoid getting into trouble. They're unfaithful to do the work when no one is watching them. That's why they're wary . . . always watching out for their superiors and others . . . to make sure they're "not caught" not working. They may be safe and mindful of the quality of their work, but they manifest a real lack of concern for the production goal. They simply don't care to reach it . . . or doing their part in helping their crew reach it. They want to "Cadillac" while their coworkers carry the brunt of the work. They care little for their coworkers.

4. **"Wandering birds": Roaming workers.** These are the *"disappearers" in the workplace*. When no one is looking, they'll try to "steal away," to roam the workplace. They'll try to "sneak off" without being seen . . . by their superiors or others . . . to enter other work areas, to converse with other workers. Before you know it, they've "disappeared" . . . from their work area. The next thing you know, their superiors are asking you, "Where is so-and-so?" They may do the work when they're in their respective work area, but they'll take the first chance they get to get out of their work area . . . to go somewhere else in the workplace.

4 Facts of Success for Safety Talks

1. **Safety talks should consist of *correct information*.** *Get your facts right!* Do your homework. Research your safety topic. Look it up and understand it. You cannot *explain* what you do not *understand*. Know what you're talking about. This will give you a good measure of confidence in delivering your message on safety. Correct information empowers your message.

2. **Safety talks should be *delightful to listen to*.** They challenge you to be creative. The real challenge is in the *presentation*, not the *preparation*. Make your message as interesting as you possibly can. Boredom will zap your message of the power to inspire your

audience. A boring message is a *dead* message. A dead message can't inspire anyone. But a *lively* message will definitely inspire your audience! Make your message enjoyable!

3. **Safety talks should *persuade people to be safe.*** *Persuasion is the real power of a really successful safety message.* People will remember what you said. Therefore, they will remember to be safe. You put something on their minds . . . much like *imprinting* it on their minds. An *imprint* about safety on the mind may very well prevent an *incident* of a worker who was mindful of what you said.

4. **Safety talks should *affect the soul.*** They should "hit home." They should touch the heart. People are human beings. Human beings have hearts. Hearts can be *touched . . . for good.* An affected soul or touched heart is the wonderful proof of a successful safety message. A successful safety message just may *save someone's life.* Take your safety talk *seriously.* It is okay to add the element of humor, but the main purpose is to *encourage* people to be safe, not *entertain* them . . . that they leave laughing and not thoughtful or intent on being safe.

In Safe M.O.D.E.

● Safety truth:

> Your ***despite*** for being safe can lead to your ***destruction*** . . . for not being safe.

Using the word *MODE* as an acronym, I let each letter stand for the following:

Manner
Of
Daily
Exhortation

It should be the manner of all to exhort one another every workday. Every workday poses a real challenge to be safe.

To be safe should be the personal goal of each employee, who reports to work.

The manner of daily exhortation should be manifested in the workplace, from workday to workday . . . from work shift to work shift . . . . from worker to worker.

This noble manner should never be lost.

It should never become a *lost art* in the "museum" of the workplace.

To exhort means "to urge."

The company should urge its chain of command at each of its divisions to keep the very topic of safety *hot*.

The chain of command should urge the supervisors, who oversee crews in the workplace, to exhort their respective crews regarding being safe.

Crewmembers should urge one another to be safe . . . and to readily address or report:

- Unsafe *conduct*
- Unsafe *conditions*

Workers are people.
People are precious.
Precious is of great value.
You are of great value!
Never take your real worth as a human being for granted.

Knowing the true value of human life should be enough to make you urge your fellow workers to be safe.

Safety is a solemn message that must be proclaimed in and out of every season of the workplace: You should proclaim it when workers want to hear it. You should proclaim it when workers don't want to hear it.

Safety must be a constant message.

4 Very Effective Ways to Urge Workers to Be Safe

1. **Urge them by ARGUMENT.** An argument is a *discussion* that involves opposing points. To get people to "see the light," you have to take time to deal with them by debate. Debate safety matters. Respectfully hear others' points and powerfully present yours. Take the power of argument. Show them the error of their thinking and

reasoning. Show them the weakness of their points. Magnify the strength of your points. *Convince them to convert them.* People are "reasoning machines." Reason with them. Have *good understanding* of the safety topic. Defeat all their points of opposition. Win them over to being safe . . . and to willingly accept/adopt safe practices.

2. **Urge them by ADMONITION.** Admonition is cautionary advice or warning. The company . . . along with its chain of command . . . wields the power to reprove workers for unsafe conduct; however, they should reprove them *gently but earnestly.* They should determine to *get their point across* . . . to the person they may be having a problem with . . . being safe. They should *caution* them through advice, but they should also *correct* them of any erroneous ways. Moreover, they should *warn* them, but they should also *work to encourage them* . . . to be safe.

3. **Urge them by ADVICE.** Advice is opinion about what could or should be done about a situation or problem. Basically, it is counsel. Counsel them about their safety situation. If an employee has a problem with safety, he should be *counseled according to his conduct.* His conduct should be the main focus . . . because his conduct is *what he actually does.* What he actually does will reflect safe performance or unsafe performance of his job. So his conduct is a key concern. Advice is an effective tool of improvement. There's always room for improvement . . . in the working life of a worker.

4. **Urge them by APPEAL.** Appeal is an *urgent request.* Learn to urgently request fellow employees to stop doing something the way they're doing it, because of the real potential danger it may possess. Don't be afraid to approach people in the workplace, and to say what's on your mind . . . regarding safety and what you see. Your *determined silence* can prove to be their *death sentence.* Be courageous to appeal to safety violators . . . simply because *YOU CARE.* The *consequence* of your bold action to appeal to them should not be outweighed by your *concern* for their very safety.

SAFETY COUNSEL FOR YOU TO CONSIDER

- Your *love of life* should become a kind of worldwide vision, to have *love for your fellow man*. Your fellow man can be your fellow worker.
- Take the first step to *work safe*. Take the second step to *watch out* for them you work with.
- It is not enough to *hear* instruction on how to be safe. You have to *heed* it.
- No one can *promise* you a safe shift. You simply must *practice* the rules of being safe.
- Safety violation is *real proof* that someone is not a *really safe worker*.
- A daydreamer is *blind* for the duration of his daydreaming. His mind is *blank* for the period of his unawareness.
- Regarding safety, *investigate* what is suspect to you; and, *interrogate* who is suspect to you. Don't let suspects off the hook so easily. You may be letting a safety matter go unattended.
- *Share* your thoughts on safety. *Show* your concern for safety. Be a voice for safety . . . in your workplace.
- If you fail to make yourself *an example* of workplace safety, the company just might make *an example* out of you.
- If you don't *heed* Safety's voice . . . no matter through whom . . . you'll *have* an incident . . . in due time.

6

Wearing "Work Clothes" of Common Sense: Use 100% of It!

● Safety truth:

> *Where there is no **exercise** of common sense there will be **expectation** of avoidable incidents.*

Common sense is possessed by all.
All don't always use it.
When people fail to use it, it can become the birthplace for mistakes.

✒ *Stupid mistakes can spell stupendous destruction!*

A safe workplace depends very heavily upon common sense.
Common sense is a worker's greatest tool.
When the greatest tool isn't used, the greatest incidents can take place.
Without this great tool, a safe workplace cannot be successfully built . . . and excitingly maintained.

Building the "House": A Two-Dimensional Approach

● Safety truth:

*A **workplace** is only as safe as its **workers**. Its workers are only as safe as they want to be.*

A steel mill sees itself as a *family.*
A family consists of *members.*
Members of a family are what workers of a steel mill are considered.
Moreover, a family lives in a *house.*
A house where a family lives is the ideal picture for a workplace where people work.
To build the "house" for a steel mill family is to build *the workplace.*
The workplace should be built from a two-dimensional approach.
The place where one works (or is employed) is his "home."

1. Building a "Safe Home"

The workplace should be "built" or made a "safe home." A "safe home" is a *safe workplace*. A safe workplace consists of safe workers. Safe workers are what the company should continually push for them to be . . . and take necessary actions to enforce their safety. A safe workplace has:

- ✓ Guards (in every possible place)
- ✓ Chains (to prevent unauthorized entry)
- ✓ Shields (of all sorts)
- ✓ Warning signs
- ✓ Cameras (strategically placed)
- ✓ Job-safety manuals/methods
- ✓ Safety meetings (periodically scheduled)

A *safe* workplace possesses the very first principle to be a *successful* workplace. Safety is the key to keep the workplace in position to reach its safety goal and be a safe place to work.

2. *Building a "Sweet Home"*

The workplace should be "built" or made a "sweet home." A "sweet home" is a pleasant place. A pleasant place consists of pleasant people. Pleasant people collectively create a pleasant atmosphere.

The workplace should be "home" to you.

Moreover, it should be "home, sweet home" to you.

Pleasant people make unpleasant work bearable.

A pleasant workplace is, indeed, a workplace to be proud of.

To build a pleasant place to work, the company cannot afford to tolerate people with bad attitudes.

People with bad attitudes are as apples with worms.

Apples with worms aren't fit for food.

Likewise, people with bad attitudes aren't fit for a pleasant workplace. *A bad attitude renders an unpleasant employee.* An unpleasant employee will be a source of negative energy in the workplace. Negative energy in the workplace will destroy the possibility of a pleasant workplace. That's why the company must courageously deal with bad attitudes. Bad attitudes are seeds for an unpleasant workplace. The workplace doesn't make itself. The workers make the workplace . . . what it is . . . the result of which can be either a good image or a bad image.

A Spiritual Viewpoint:
Seeing People in the Workplace for What They Are

● Safety truth:

> *Luck is unreliable. It won't always be there for you. Caution is one of your most reliable assets.* **Caution** *causes* **consideration.**

From a spiritual viewpoint, I've seen four kinds of people in the workplace for what they are, regarding being safe.

Being safe is a basic responsibility . . . of workers.
- ▶ Workers are *expected* to work safe.
- ▶ Workers must *exercise common sense.*

Sometimes, safety violators are lucky. They might *get away* unscathed or only with minor bruises.

Other times, safety violators might *get caught* . . . in their safety violation, paying a pretty good price for it.

Here are four kinds of people in the workplace I've seen for what they are, in regard to safety and safety's observance and its overbearing violators.

1. *"Signs."* I call people in the workplace, who've suffered serious injuries from safety violation, "signs" because their unfortunately left marks of regretful injury can be *seen* by others. A missing finger . . . a permanent limp . . . a scarred hand . . . a disfigured face . . . are just a terrible few.
2. *"Wonders."* I call people in the workplace, who arouse astonishment of other workers by their astounding feats, "wonders." It's a wonder they didn't get seriously hurt . . . or killed . . . in pulling those unsafe stunts.
3. *"Miracles."* I call people in the workplace, who've committed safety violation and survived when death seemed sure, "miracles." It's a miracle they didn't die in what seemed sure death . . . for them. Somehow, they escaped death. They're walking miracles in the workplace. They should have been fatalities in the workplace . . . for their major safety violation.
4. *"Gifts."* I call people in the workplace, who have *special abilities* to teach, instruct, and inspire others to be safe, "gifts." The company should appreciate its "gifts." These special types of people are rarely found in the workplace. *Motivation must have its motivational speakers.*

As can be plainly seen from this spiritual viewpoint, the majority of people who work in the workplace, are safe workers.

As safe workers *increase,* workplace incidents *decrease.*

They diminish because they're dominantly avoidable.

Common sense is a common cure for continually growing incidents.

A Real Reason Why Safety Talks May Not Benefit You

● Safety truth:

*When safety is **talked**, it is **taught**.*

Safety talks introduce *teachable moments.*
They empower employees with *specific information* they need to know.
They are effective tools in the toolbox of safety.
Steel mills that have *safety goals* will have *safety talks*.

A real reason why safety talks may not *benefit* you is that you don't *believe* they can.
When you don't believe they can, you won't take real interest in them . . . as they're being delivered.
The power of safety talks is in *information form.*
Information is power.
Safety talks do a powerful lot of good . . . in helping to keep workers safe. But:

● *Workers must **accept** them . . . as true.*
● *Workers must **apply** them . . . to benefit from them.*

Safety talks won't do you any good if you don't believe they can do you any good.
Check your attitude towards safety talks.
If you *despise* them, you will *deprive* yourself of their preserving power.
Their preserving power is *experienced* in heeding them and acting in accordance with their safe instructions.

Safety talks aren't wastes of time. They are *worthy investments.*
It is when you *receive* them that you can *reap* their benefits. Their key benefits are:

- Good understanding
- Guidance
- Guarding

Safety talks will guard or protect you as you allow them to lead you.

To lead you, you must follow the advice or counsel they convey to you.

You should look in the mirror. Seeing yourself, you see someone who's responsible for being safe.

Being safe is a *responsibility* that some workers sometimes unwisely ignore.

3 Key Things You Should Expect to Receive from Safety Talks

1. **When listening to safety talks, you should expect to receive INFORMATION.** Information is a collection of facts. Facts are based on real occurrences. *Information is an ideal cure for ignorance.* Ignorance can prove deadly. You need to be informed. You need to be *in the know* . . . of what's happened or is happening or will be happening . . . in the workplace. Information can *warn* you of what you *specifically* need to watch out for, in your place of work. Information is a tremendous tool to heighten your awareness of safety-related concerns. It is crucial you pay very close attention to safety talks, as they can warn you of unsuspecting dangers and help preserve your extreme respect for what can potentially harm you.
2. **When listening to safety talks, you should expect to receive INSTRUCTION.** Instruction is the practice or profession of an instructor. An instructor may be procured by the company, to instruct you in how to do certain things the safe way, and to warn you of real potential dangers you may be unaware of. Steel mill companies will host *different* instructors, to give their employees *different kinds of* information, insight, ideas, and invaluable examples and experiences. On this wise, the company goes out of its way, to keep its workers safe. You should pay very close attention to instructors, who can show you how to keep safe and to preserve your very life, in all kinds of instances. *Where there is no instruction there will be ignorance.* Again, ignorance can prove deadly.

3. **When listening to safety talks, you should expect to receive INSPIRATION.** Inspiration is the quality of inspiring. Safety talks should be purposefully designed to stimulate you to safe action. You should expect to be *motivated* . . . by them. Inspiration is the "crème de la crème" of safety talks. It is the superlative of safety talks. When workers are inspired . . . to keep safe . . . by safety talks, those very safety talks prove effectual and wonderfully successful. *An inspiring safety talk is always a winner!* It sets people "on fire" to be safe. People appreciate inspiration. They appreciate *being inspired.* Being inspired is a beautiful thing. Inspiration is ideally what a workplace which has a safety problem, needs. If a workplace keeps "dropping the ball" of being safe, it may need a "dose" of inspiration. Inspiration will bring the workers "to life," sort of speak. It will quicken a genuine sense of concern for safety, in them. You should pay very close attention to inspirers . . . as "precious," for the fact that not all safety-talkers are inspiring. *Seize every instance to be wonderfully inspired . . . to be safe!*

The Heart: Having a "Secret Chamber" and a "Secret Counselor" Within

● Safety truth:

> Safety **must be** more than a thought. It **must become** an action.

When workers stray away from being safe, it is because they err in *their heart.*

Their heart is a secret chamber, where they convene with themselves . . . where they talk to themselves . . . about what they *intend* to do.

The Bible has this to say about the heart:

> *The heart is deceitful above all things, and desperately wicked: who can know it?*
>
> —JEREMIAH 17:9

You should know . . . and understand . . . two real facts about the heart:

1. The heart is *deceitful.* It is given to deceiving. Your heart will *deceive you.* It will mislead you. It will lead you astray. When it comes to being safe, don't trust your heart. Rather, trust the safety rules. The safety rules are developed from investigation and study of past incidents of real occurrences in the workplace. They are the results of lessons learned from incidents of individual workers . . . whether from property damages, injuries, or fatalities.
2. The heart is *desperately wicked.* This means there's no cure for its wicked condition. If you listen to and follow the advice of a wicked counselor, you will have a wicked experience. A wicked experience won't be good or favorable for you. It will be bad or unfortunate for you. Think about safety. Think about the safety rules. Ponder the practices and principles of safety. But don't make the mistake of letting your *untrustworthy* heart lead you away from the protective benefits they offer.

Convene with your coworker.

Introduce your intentions to him. Allow him to examine them. He may *detect* error in your judgment or flaws in your most carefully laid plans . . . to accomplish your assigned tasks.

You're not necessarily seeking his *approval* but rather his *opinion.*

Consider the opinions of others. Learn to see things from their perspective. *More eyes can cover more areas.* For that there's safety in numbers, you can find safety in many perspectives of people who see what you may not, and therefore can bring you valuable awareness.

Never lose sight of the fact that safety is a *team effort.* Learn to get other workers *involved* concerning your ideas and your intentions. *Humility gives you access to the valuable perspectives of others.*

Knowing the Ways of Doing Your Work

● Safety truth:

> *If you don't **understand** how to be safe, then you won't **stand a chance** at being safe.*

You have your ways of doing your work.
Your ways of doing your work are either safe or unsafe.
You need to *know* if they're safe or unsafe.
You can know if they're safe or unsafe by:

- *Personal experience.* You learn what is safe or unsafe by what you live through. They are lessons to last you a lifetime. If experience is the best teacher, then your workplace is a type of life class you should not make light of.
- *Personal observation.* You become aware of things through your careful and directed attention. You notice what is safe and what is unsafe. You commit what you come to realize, to your memory. This helps you to abide by safety rules and regulations. You've *seen* what can happen . . . if you execute a certain action or follow a certain course of doing something.
- *Personal study.* You inquire into real events in the workplace. You take it upon yourself to investigate incidents of others. You apply yourself to learning from those incidents. You apply your mind purposefully to acquire understanding of what happened, to whom it happened, why it happened, and how it can happen *to you.*

Know the ways of doing your work. Don't be "in the dark" about how you go about doing your job. Consider the courses of action you follow. Analyze the actions you take. Understand the path of your performance you always take.

Be willing . . . and wise . . . to:

▶ ***Abandon*** *unsafe practices, and*
▶ ***Adopt*** *safe practices . . . of others.*

Your safety depends on your safe ways . . . of doing things.

Your safe ways will help keep you secure in the course of accomplishing your work.

Your work involves not only your assigned tasks but also your personal responsibility to be safe.

Discerning the Deceitfulness of Safety Violation: Don't Be Fooled!

● Safety truth:

> ***Violation*** *of safety rules can lead to **violence** done to your physical body.*

With steel mills, safety violation is a major concern.

A major concern will keep the company on pins and needles. Workplace safety keeps the company in a state of anxious suspense or nervous anticipation. The company is always "worried about" the safety of its workers.

Workers have to realize that they can become *hardened* (in their hearts) against safety rules through the deceitfulness of safety violation.

Safety violation will *deceive* you. It will make you feel it is okay to do what you well know is unsafe. Repeats of safety violation will reinforce your belief that nothing will happen to you. Don't be fooled!

You must discern the deceitfulness of safety violation. You have to recognize how it can really mislead you to think that you will be alright when you violate safety. The more you practice something, the more you become *relaxed* with doing it. When you relax, you *ease up* on your guard. When this happens, you begin to grow careless.

Carelessness is a common cause of many incidents.

Don't become careless. Stay cautious!

Understand your safety violation will be a *deceiver* to you. Don't trust it. Belief that you will be safe can be your undoing.

Significance of the Seventh Day: The Soul Factor

● Safety truth:

> A ***tired body*** is a ***ticking time bomb*** for an incident. It is just a matter of time . . . before something bad happens.

It is very interesting to note what Genesis 2:2 says, which states:

> *And on the seventh day God ended His work which He had made; and He rested on the seventh day from all His work which He had made.*

The seventh day bears significance because of the *secret benefit* it contains.

That secret benefit is *rejuvenation.*
Rejuvenation is restoration to youthful vigor.
Rejuvenation is the result of rest.
When you rest, you rejuvenate your body.

But more than your body is rejuvenated. Your *sense of safety* is also rejuvenated. Your awareness . . . of where you are . . . is significantly heightened. Mental clarity is key to being focused. Your mind must be alert for you to be safe.

What I refer to "the seventh day" is simply the last day of your workweek.

A week consists of *seven days.*
Seven days are your allotted time to do your work.
Your work has to have a *rest period.*
A rest period is required for rejuvenation.
Typically, people work *six days* and rest on the *seventh day.*
This produces a common life schedule of:

◆ Six days of *work,* and
◆ One day of *worship.*

Worship gives a divine benefit . . . of spiritual rest.
Spiritual rest is for your *soul*.
Physical rest is for your *body*.
People who're tired in their soul are just as incident-prone as those that are tired in their bodies.
Don't make light of the soul factor.
If your soul isn't rejuvenated:

- You may not be *mindful* to be safe.
- You may not be *willing* to be alert.
- You may not be *emotionally* fit . . . to be in the workplace.

You must recognize the fact that not only is your *body* in the workplace but also your *soul*.
Your soul is where you have your *sense of safety*.
Your sense of safety is critical. You must make sure it isn't *dulled* for lack of rest.
Lack of rest means no rejuvenation . . . and moreover, spiritual rejuvenation.

Limit a Certain Day to Rest!

● Safety truth:

Your common sense is your life tool with which to make intelligent decisions. Intelligent decisions are **seeds** *for* **safe actions.**

A day to rest is a *period of twenty-four hours* to cease from work.
Work takes its toll on your body and soul.
Your body and soul should receive a whole day's break from the brutal demands work heaps upon them.
For this solemn reason, you should limit a certain day to rest.
You should make it a *law of your life*.
Your body and soul are your personal responsibilities: Take very good care of them. Your very health depends on it.

- A healthy body won't do you much good if you have no healthy soul.
- A healthy soul won't do you much good if you have no healthy body.

One without the other will render you *incapacitated*. You will be disabled to a certain degree.

Your body and soul *work together.*
They work together to produce for you a *healthy life.*
A healthy life belongs to a healthy worker.
A healthy worker is the "cell" of the "body" of a healthy workplace.
A healthy workplace has the golden promise of being a safe workplace.

Laying the Foundation for a Safe Workplace

● Safety truth:

> *Safety must be a **firm establishment** in your day-to-day work routines, or you'll have a **frequent occurrence** of incidents on your job.*

A house has to be built.
It cannot be built until its foundation is laid.
The foundation supports the house.
Similarly, a safe workplace has to be *built.*
But before it can be built, its *foundation* has to be laid.

↳ *Where there is no **foundation** there will be no **firm support!***

A safe workplace needs a firm support, so it doesn't fall away . . . or cease to exist.

Question: *What is the foundation for a safe workplace?*
Answer: *A safety program.*

A safety program must be put in place, whereupon a safe workplace can be built . . . or beautifully realized.

> A safety program is a system of *projects*.
> Projects are planned or devised by the company.
> The company perceives the need for safety projects.
> Safety projects are what a safe workplace basically consists of.
> Safety projects should be seen throughout the workplace. They should be seen in every work area.
> Safety projects are *visible signs* of the company's concern for the safety of its workers.

Laying the foundation of a safe workplace is simply accomplished by putting a safety program in place.

☙ *Where there is no **safety program** there cannot be a **safe workplace!***

The safety program must be *enforced*.
The company must compel observance of it or obedience to it.
Failure to enforce it will render it a *weak foundation*.

A weak foundation cannot support a safe place to work . . . for long. It is a matter of time before it finally gives away. Once it gives away, a surprisingly quick influx of incidents can be expected.

There is what I call "termites" that will "eat away" the "foundation" for a safe workplace. The company needs to be aware of them. Let's identify some of them:

- *The "termite" of despite.* Despite of employees will destroy the real effectiveness of a safety program by virtue of them regarding it with contempt or scorn. For a safety program to be successful, it must command the respect of employees.
- *The "termite" of disinterest.* Disinterest (lack of interest) of employees will destroy the real effectiveness of a safety program by virtue of them regarding it as unworthy of their interest or concern. For a safety program to be successful, it must command the interest of employees.

- *The "termite" of disagreement.* Disagreement of employees will destroy the real effectiveness of a safety program by virtue of them failing to correspond to the company's diligent efforts to keep them safe. Having a differing opinion, they should humbly accept the fact that the company is "in charge," and that what it says goes and what it wants done should be done . . . for fear of disciplinarian action or discharge. For a safety program to be successful, it must command the approval of employees.
- *The "termite" of dissatisfaction.* Dissatisfaction of employees will destroy the real effectiveness of a safety program by virtue of them being disappointed with the company (for whatever reason), that they could care less for the safety program the company has put in place . . . and may even ignore it. For a safety program to be successful, it must command the appreciation of employees.

Shame on You!

● Safety truth:

> **Proud workers** can pose a **problem** for pursuing and achieving the safety goal.

Pride of workers can get them into trouble . . . especially with the company.

The company has zero tolerance for insubordination. It expects firmly for workers to do what they're asked to do . . . as long as it doesn't involve bodily harm or jeopardizes them in any way.

When workers let their pride reign against the will or wishes of the company, their pride will prove to be the key that will unlock for them the door of *shame.*

Shame is the reward of pride.

Shame is a painful emotion caused by a strong sense of embarrassment.

Embarrassment is not the intent of the company. But workers can *feel embarrassed* before fellow workers, when the company powerfully asserts itself, showing no signs of intimidation . . . of its hired hands.

> ℞ *When you refuse to **pocket your pride**, you will **pay the price** of shame!*

You should wisely make humility your quality of choice.
- ▶ Humility *protects from* shame.
- ▶ Humility *promotes to* honor.

Humility is your friend, not your enemy. The company expects it. You should have it . . . or acquire it, if you don't have it.

Know that *humility* is just as important [to the company] as *ability*.
Ability and *arrogance* aren't a popular combination with the company.

So what say I to these things?
Shame on you . . . for being too proud to comply with the company!
The company cannot profit from your pride.
You yourself cannot profit from your pride.
What you cannot profit from you should lose.
What you cannot profit from is a poor investment!

The Golden Advantage of Humility

● Safety truth:

> Your ***pride*** *can cause you to forfeit **protection*** *of what you're unwilling to hear and heed.*

At the beginning of this book, I humbly . . . yet boldly . . . declared the great importance of Workplace Wisdom.

As life plainly teaches, wisdom is not found with foolish people; nor is it found with proud people.

Wisdom is found with humble people.

Humble people have a heart that's receptive of wisdom. They are the ones who will:

- *Hear* it . . .
- *Heed* it . . .
- *Have* it committed to their memory . . .

The golden advantage of humility is the ability to receive Wisdom. Wisdom is safety's ultimate necessity.

↬ *Where there is no **wisdom** there is a **workplace** where foolish practices flourish and incidents increase!*

If knowledge is *power,* then Wisdom is *royalty!*
A safe worker must first be a *wise* worker.
A wise worker knows how to be safe and is heedful of consequences for being unsafe.
The humble worker is receptive of wise instruction . . . on how to be safe. Wise instruction is pleasant to his soul.

Here are some things you can do, to help you be . . . or become . . . a humble worker:

1. *Pocket* your pride.
2. *Put* a restraint on yourself from associating with rebel workers.
3. *Practice* talking less and listening more.
4. *Prepare* to be instructed by others . . . when you come to work.
5. *Prove* your humility by your compliance.
6. *Perform* your job with a smile!
7. *Plan* to fulfill every assigned task exactly as instructed, offering no excuses.
8. *Pleasure* yourself by taking joy in teamwork.
9. *Pin* your mistakes on yourself.

Always remember that humility is the honorable path to being or becoming a wise worker.

- A wise worker is the first stage of being a safe worker.
- A wise worker *listens and learns.*
- A wise worker increases his safety knowledge.
- A wise worker is empowered to equip others.
- A wise worker is a *crown jewel* of the workplace.

Humility is the doorstep to honor.

Pride prevents your promotion . . . when the company would honor you by promoting you.

Never underestimate the awesome power of Humility!

Never forget its golden advantage!

Owning a "GPS": A Secret of a Safe Worker

● Safety truth:

*You're only **as safe** as you're **attentive** to be safe.*

Being a safe worker myself, I've discovered I have a "GPS" within me. It's not instinct. However, it is a "navigational system" of an intangible type, which *guides* me [my thoughts and actions] in the workplace.

This intangible navigational system to which I refer is known as *integrity*.

Integrity is steadfast adherence to a strict moral or ethical code.

In the case of safety, it is steadfast adherence to a Safety Code.

A Safety Code shouldn't be limited to steel mills.

Every workplace should have a Safety Code.

A Safety Code is a systematic collection of regulations and rules of safety procedure or safe conduct.

A safe worker is a *person of integrity* . . . as far as steadfast adherence to a Safety Code goes.

▶ Integrity is a *moral excellence.*
▶ Integrity is a *main quality.*

You should make integrity one of your main qualities.

You should have rigid adherence to safety rules and regulations.

Rigid adherence to safety rules and regulations will *guide* you in the safe way of doing things, in the workplace.

It will help keep you from *going astray* . . . from the safe way of doing things.

↯ *Your **mind** must be **made up** . . . to be safe!*

A person of integrity doesn't *accept bribes*.

A safe worker having integrity (steadfast adherence to safety rules and regulations) doesn't *yield to temptations . . . to take shortcuts . . . or the easy but dangerous way.*

Integrity is a very powerful weapon against incidents.

Integrity carries a sense of commitment. If you can stay committed to being safe, guess what? In all likelihood, you *will be safe!*

Agreed??

Here are some personal questions by which you can check yourself for the main quality of integrity:

1. Are you safe when no one else is around or looking at you?
2. Are you safety-conscious during break time, at your shift's end, or when you're out of the workplace?
3. Are you aware of your surroundings during a conversation or some other kind of communication, while on the work floor?
4. Are you easily distracted (by whatever or whoever) from what you're doing?
5. Are you forgetful to reorient yourself when you return to your work area, for example, after break?
6. Are you perceptive of potential dangers that may lurk in the workplace? Can you recognize them?
7. Are you safe because you have to be or because you want to be?
8. Are you too proud to listen to coworkers, who may see you doing something potentially unsafe and take the time to bring it to your attention?

Safety and *superegos* are misfits . . . for each other.

What are you willing to give in exchange for your well-being and your very life?

Incidents can be costly.

Incidents happen to many workers who lack integrity.

Don't become a statistic!

Be a shining example of workplace safety!

Integrity can help you shine!

Steadfast adherence to safety rules and regulations can reward you with genuine joy!

Perceiving a "Protective Angel"

● Safety truth:

> A workplace has its **vision** of safety . . . and its **violations** of safety.

Never underestimate the vital importance of doing things the right way.

Doing things the right way *protects* you . . . or keeps you safe . . . in the workplace.

The workplace is where you should *perceive* doing things the right way as a "protective angel."

A protective angel *protects*.

Doing things the right way *protects* . . . you.

You should know that when you don't do something the right way, you render your "protective angel" useless . . . to you.

As long as you do things the right way, you put your "protective angel" to work . . . for you.

It only stands to reason then that to do things the *wrong* way is to perceive a "death angel."

A death angel *brings death*.

Doing things the wrong way . . . the unsafe way . . . will *bring death* . . . to you.

You have to understand your safety depends on the kinds of choices you make.

The kinds of choices you make determine the kinds of actions you take.

Your actions are *seeds* . . . for either your *preservation* or your *destruction*.

Your destruction will be your total ruin.

Total ruin is what many unsafe workers reap.

You will be *tempted* to do the wrong thing.

Temptation presents you with *a choice*.

That choice will be to:
▶ *Yield to* the temptation, or
▶ *Resist* it.

Your "protective angel" cannot protect you if you yield to the temptation to do things the wrong way.

Your "protective angel" can only protect you if you resist the temptation to do things the wrong way.

Use your common sense!
Your common sense is your life tool.
Your life tool is to *serve* you.
You build a safe workday by using your common sense.

👉 *Common incidents flourish in the absence of common sense!*

A vital key to being a safe worker is *consistency*.
Consistency requires commitment.
Commitment causes for determination.
Determination is proof of concern for personal safety.
Personal safety requires diligent effort.
Diligent effort is given by a responsible worker.
A responsible worker is the "basic unit" of a really safe workplace.

7 Rules for Being a Responsible Worker

1. **The Rule of CONFORMATION.** A responsible worker *conforms to* or complies with all Company rules and regulations. The rules and regulations are not only for *smooth* operation in the workplace but also *safe* operation in the workplace.
2. **The Rule of CAUTION.** A responsible worker is a *cautious* worker. He thinks before he acts to avoid danger or harm. If you're not careful, you will allow routine to rob you of your focus. Don't let doing the same things day in and day out cause you to lose your focus. If you're not thinking or paying attention before you act, then you are not focused—and you need to get refocused.
3. **The Rule of CONFIRMATION.** A responsible worker does not assume; he *confirms*. He doesn't assume anything is right. He takes the time to make sure it's right! There's an old saying that goes, "Assumption is the mother of all mess-ups."

4. **The Rule of CORRECTION.** A responsible worker stands to be corrected, if he is in error or is doing something wrong or the wrong way. This causes for true humility. A proud worker will manifest the wrong attitude and can make it hard for others. It's always a good practice to listen and get a good understanding.
   When it comes to machines, if something can't be fixed, it needs to be replaced. The same principle can be applied to a proud worker: If he can't be corrected, he needs to be replaced; not only for his own safety but also for the safety of others.
5. **The Rule of COOPERATION.** A responsible worker is *cooperative*. He works together with others toward a common goal. Each workday presents a set production goal that they're to work together toward reaching. If someone isn't pulling his load, then that means extra work is being directed to someone else . . . who's already working. When extra work is heaped upon someone else who's already doing what he's supposed to do, it increases his risk for having an incident. If a worker is dodging work, then he's not cooperating. It's not only *unfair* to those working; it's also *unsafe* for them.
6. **The Rule of COMMUNICATION.** A responsible person *communicates* with others. He exchanges thoughts or ideas, messages, or other work-related information, with whom he works. When you communicate with your coworkers, you play your part in making sure others are "in the know." Communication helps to put everyone on the same page. Miscommunication ranks very high with other things that contribute to most incidents in the workplace.
7. **The Rule of CONSIDERATION.** A responsible worker considers others he works with. Consideration of other workers is a huge part of teamwork and is going the extra mile to help prevent job incidents.

PERSONAL SAFETY: A "PERSONAL WORKOUT"

● Safety truth:

> *Personal safety not only requires your **attention;** it also requires your **action!***

Personal fitness is a personal responsibility.
It is your responsibility to take good care of yourself . . . your body.
Personal workout is the means to the end of personal fitness.
You have to work out to be . . . and to stay . . . fit.

Seeing this from a Safety standpoint, personal safety is a personal responsibility.
It is your responsibility to take good care of yourself safe-wise . . . or to be safe.
When seen in this light, it becomes clear that personal safety is a "personal workout."
You have to "work out" your own safety . . . with great respect for what has the potential to harm . . . and even kill . . . you.
Personal safety has to be "worked out" in your life . . . daily.
Just as being physically fit doesn't just happen—you have to work out—being safe doesn't just happen—you have to "work out."
To work out personal safety means to ***accomplish*** it by work or effort.
You have to "put in the work" to be safe.
You have to make the effort to be safe . . . continually.

Unsafe people are as unfit people, who don't work out.
Unless you ***see*** your own safety as a "personal workout," you will be ***blind*** to the truth that you must make the effort to be safe . . . at all times.
What you don't see yourself as, you won't strive to be.
If you don't see yourself as being safe, then you won't make the honest effort to be safe . . . continually.
Personal safety is a "personal workout!"
Be wise for yourself to get in the daily habit of working out your own safety.

Personal safety begins with the person.
Therefore, your own safety begins with *you!*

THINKERS: THE IMPORTANCE OF BEING THE RIGHT KIND

● Safety truth:

*Your safety encompasses your **mind** . . . and your **motions**.*

Basically, there are two kinds of people in this world: negative people and positive people.

People are *thinkers*.

Negative people are negative thinkers; positive people are positive thinkers.

As a person, you are a thinker.

The important question is: *"What kind of thinker are you?"*

Negative thinkers mind negative things. They only care about what's negative.

Positive thinkers mind positive things. They're mainly concerned about what's positive.

But here's the significant difference between the two:

Negative Thinkers

Negative thinkers experience "death" in their minds.

They have dead ideas, dead plans, dead dreams, etc.

Their negative thinking takes the "life" (liveliness, vitality, animation) out of their minds.

Negative people aren't dreamers and doers.

They're as *dead people*.

Dead people have *no hope*.

Negative thinkers have no hope of achievement in life.

Their negative thinking *destroys* the possibility of personal success.

Positive Thinkers

Positive thinkers experience "life" and "peace" in their minds.
They have lively ideas, lively plans, lively dreams, etc.
Their positive thinking preserves the "life" (liveliness, vitality, animation) of their minds.
Positive thinkers are dreamers and doers.
They're as *living people.*
People who're alive *have hope.*
Positive thinkers have hope of achievement in life.
Their positive thinking *preserves* the possibility of personal success.

Plus, positive thinkers have a bonus: They have *peace of mind.*
Their minds aren't troubled by the trials of life.
They don't let life get them down.
Positive thinkers are *mental survivors.*

- They survive *bad news.*
- They survive *life's obstacles.*
- They survive *their failures.*
- They survive *discouragement.*
- They survive *temptations to give up.*

I hope you can plainly see the importance of being the right kind of thinker in this world.
This world isn't known for being sympathetic.
You have to stand strong and firm . . . and being a positive thinker will help you to do so.
Whereas the negative thinker sees only a *hopeless situation,* the positive thinker looks for a *hopeful solution.*

Be encouraged to be a positive thinker!
Positive thinking puts you on the path to possible solutions!
Life will bring its challenges to bear; but when it does, you bring the power of your positive thinking to bear!
A positive thinker is as a bold lion.
So be a bold lion in life! Don't let life's challenges intimidate you!

- *Stand your ground!*
- *Stand strong!*
- *Stand firm in purpose!*

If you don't stand, you will fail . . . throughout your life.
Be encouraged!
Don't accept failure! Let success only satisfy you!

THINK SAFETY!!!

SAFETY COUNSEL FOR YOU TO CONSIDER

- If something happens to you in the workplace, *investigate* the happening and *interrogate* yourself. If you don't understand what happened . . . to you . . . then you won't be able to explain it to others.
- Your *involvement* in an *incident* will be looked upon as a "field" wherefrom others can "glean" knowledge . . . of what actually happened.
- What you do not *remember* you won't be able to *report*. Commit to memory what happens . . . so you'll be able to recall it.
- If you *dare,* your safety violation might be a *snare!*
- The safety violator is deserving of *punishment* . . . and is robbed of *peace.*
- Every worker should know that *arrogance* will keep him near an *accident.*
- When your thoughts *distract* you, they *destroy* your focus.
- If you don't *learn from* your incident, you will *live through it* again. The seed for a repeat is sown.
- Your *stubbornness* will lead to your *stupid mistakes.*
- The *safe* way you will not take will give way to the *sure* way to an incident you will have.
- Your hands are *instrumental* . . . not *indestructible.*
- Keep your eyes *peeled* for what may be *concealed!*

7

Wearing a "Shield": Trust in God as Your Personal Protection!

● Safety truth:

> Being safe doesn't involve **only you** but **others.** Others may see what's potentially harmful you may not see.

You may be able to watch out and be safe according to your own ability *to a certain extent.*

But there are real dangers which you cannot possibly guard yourself from simply because *you are human.*

Being human, your ability to keep safe is limited.

- You cannot see . . . or foresee . . . every thing that may happen to you.
- You cannot safeguard yourself from freak accidents.
- You cannot really prepare for the unexpected, though you try to expect the unexpected.
- You cannot predict the future of an incident.
- You cannot stop every thing from happening because you don't possess the power to.

For these solemnly real facts, you need a *Divine Shield.*
Proverbs 30:5 states:

Every word of God is pure: He is a SHIELD unto them that put their trust in Him.

You need to trust in God as your "Shield."

As your "Shield," God will *protect* you from "weapons" of the-humanly impossible-to guard against kind, which you may find hurled or thrusted at you . . . in the workplace.

What you should wisely do is:

- Do what you *can do* to be safe; and
- Trust God to do what you *cannot do* to be safe.

Personally, I'm a living testimony to the marvelous faithfulness of God to keep me safe in this world . . . and in the workplace.

Here are some awesome things I've learned over my working years about trusting God as my Shield . . . my Personal Protection:

1. His divine protection isn't *limited by locale*. God can . . . and will . . . keep you safe *wherever* you happen to be.
2. His divine protection isn't guaranteed when you choose to *pull foolishly dangerous stunts*. God expects you to be as safe as you possibly know how . . . and trust Him to keep you safe from what you cannot guard yourself against. Walk by *faith* . . . not in *foolishness*.
3. His divine protection isn't *dependent on other people*. God is well able to keep you safe *Himself*. However, He will *use others* in His faithfulness to keep you safe.
4. His divine protection isn't *subject to some time limit*. God will protect you for as long as you trust Him to do so.
5. His divine protection isn't *magical . . . but miraculous*. God specializes in doing the impossible . . . and that includes keeping you safe even from freak accidents.
6. His divine protection isn't *limited to **machines** but guards you against **mean men**, who desire your hurt*.
7. His divine protection isn't *suspended when you leave the workplace*. God will keep you safe beyond the workplace.

You simply cannot protect yourself from every potential danger. That's why you need God as your Personal Protection.

As your Personal Protection, He will give you confidence . . . to live your life without fear of sudden destruction . . . and to work in the workplace without fear of sudden death.

Being Safe . . . And Productive: The Twofold Revelation of the Real Workplace

● Safety truth:

> *Responsible people, who're disciplined* **to work**, *are responsible for being disciplined* **to work safe.**

The real workplace is a real world.
A real world has real events.
Real events can involve real people.
Real people are the actual workers who "inhabit the world" of the workplace.
The workplace has a twofold revelation that you should know . . . and govern yourself accordingly, in regard to it.

1. *The real workplace is a "plant."*

The real workplace is a "plant."
A plant is a *production facility*.
As a production facility, its main activity is *production*.
Production can be *dangerous work*.
Dangerous work ever reserves the real potential to result in injuries or fatalities, for the workers.
The workers **must** respect the work they do and the dangerous environment they may work in.

A plant produces fruit . . . through its branches.
Its "fruit" is its products/services.
Its "branches" are its workers.
For a plant to be really profitable, it must have *safe workers*.

Safe workers are the secret to maximization of production and minimization of incidents (property damages, injuries, and fatalities).

This is a key reason why the company should "prune" its plant (or production facility) of unsafe workers.

Unsafe workers *cost the company.*

The company cannot realize *prosperity* when the *profits* are "pierced" (or cut into) by the unforgiving "sword" of incidents.

Incidents happen to people on the job.

When people on the job keep safe, they help the company to *really profit.*

When they help the company to really profit, the company then can *reward them with raises.*

Therefore, raises are *motivating factors* for people on the job to keep safe.

Notwithstanding, safe workers will "abide" in the plant, and unsafe workers will be "cut off" from the plant.

2.   *The real workplace is a "garden."*

The real workplace is a "garden."
A garden produces *crops.*
A production facility produces *profits.*
A garden produces crops *through its plants.*
A production facility produces profits *through its workers.*
The farmer plants seeds in his garden . . . to reap harvests.
The company plants "seeds" or workers (hopefully safe ones) in its production facility, to reap "harvests" of financial profits.
The company is in business mainly to make money . . . to produce as much profits as it possibly can.

Notwithstanding, *unfavorable conditions* can affect expected harvests.
Unfavorable conditions for harvests can be:

- *Bad weather* (which can damage or destroy growing crops)
- *Basic needs unmet* (crops need water; large fields of crops need plenty of water or rain)

Similarly, unfavorable conditions for financial profits can be:

- *Bad working conditions.* These can render the workplace unsafe. An unsafe workplace is the perfect breeding ground for incidents. Incidents "damage" or "destroy" financial profits.
- *Basic personal protection.* This is workers' P.P.E. (personal protective equipment). The company must continually supply its workers with it.

Bad plants are unfavorable for good crops.
Bad "plants" or unsafe workers are unfavorable for financial profits of the company.
Therefore, safe workers will remain in the "garden" or the production facility; but unsafe workers will be "rooted out" of the "garden."
Safety is a secret to sensational profits!

Being a Wise Worker: Two Basic Ways

- Safety truth:

    *Safety has its **knowledge**. Workers should **know how** to work safe.*

I've said it before, I'll say it again: *A safe worker is a wise worker.*
A wise worker has *knowledge and understanding.*
A wise worker:
▶ *Knows* what is unsafe.
▶ *Understands* why it is unsafe . . . and the potential consequences of it.

Every worker hired by the company should have the personal quest of being a wise worker.
Here are two basic ways to be a wise worker:

1. Receive *guidance.* Learn to seek advice *about* how to be safe, *from* fellow workers who know how to do something safe. This causes for true humility. A humble person will *reach for help . . . from others.* Don't let pride keep you from reaching . . . and being safe.

2. Receive *good instruction*. All instruction isn't good. "Cease, my son, to hear the instruction that causeth to err from the words of knowledge," (Proverbs 19:27). Some workers will try to "teach" you shortcuts. Don't receive unsafe teaching. Good instruction is *safe teaching*. Safe teaching will help keep you safe . . . in the course of doing your job.

A wise worker knows how to work safe.
A wise worker knows how to teach others to work safe.
To work safe is to be the highest goal of every hired hand.
Every hired hand has to be *counseled and instructed* in how to work safe.
Therefore, the workplace must not only be a place of *employment;* it must also be a place of *empowerment.*
Empowerment is the chief aim of *education.*
Education is the essential tool to building safe workers.
Safe workers are the "building blocks" to having a safe workplace.

Being Betrayed: "Lady Luck" Will Be Unfaithful to You!

● Safety truth:

> *Your **mind** should direct the course of your **movement** in the workplace. Don't move into action until you've weighed the cost and consequence thereof.*

Luck is one of the most depended-on things to keep people safe.
The problem is that luck is as an "unfaithful woman."
An unfaithful woman cannot be trusted . . . by her husband.
It is a mistake to be married to luck!
Luck will let you down. It won't always "be there" for you.
You have to know that luck is *unfaithful.*
What is unfaithful is *untrustworthy.*
You should never trust in luck.

Some workers who "survive" their incidents . . . or get through them with only minor or no physical injuries . . . consider themselves *lucky.*

Being lucky yesterday is no guarantee you'll be lucky today.
Being lucky today is no guarantee you'll be lucky tomorrow.
Lady Luck will be unfaithful to you!

A safe worker is one who's *blameless* of safety violation. He does the right things.
The right things are the safe things.
Doing the right things *directs his way* in the workplace.
Doing the right things *leads him away from a lot of incidents . . . which he could potentially have.*

The converse is also true.
An unsafe worker is one who's *guilty* of safety violation . . . and practice of it.
He does the wrong things.
The wrong things are the unsafe things.
Doing the wrong things will cause him to have many incidents.
Many incidents will be by his own safety violation, which he may practice.

Here are several things that you should know about luck:

1. Luck is not a *person* but a *personal belief.* Many people believe in luck. That's why they consider themselves to be "lucky" when something bad doesn't happen to them.
2. Luck can be *dangerous* because it can be *deceiving.* People can seemingly "get away" so many times until they begin to erroneously believe nothing will happen to them. This, of course, strengthens their belief that they'll be just fine.
3. Luck can be the driving force that makes *disobedient workers* to become *daredevils* . . . in the workplace. It creates in them an "I'm-safe superego." Naturally, people act on what they believe. If they *believe* they'll be safe doing something unsafe, they'll *be bold* to do it.
4. Luck can *disappear* just as fast as it can *appear.* It may be with you for only a year . . . only a month . . . only a week . . . only a day . . . only an hour . . . a minute . . . only a second. Just when you think luck is *here to stay,* it may *fly away!*

Don't see yourself as *lucky.*
Rather, see yourself as *safe!*

The safety goal isn't dependent on lucky workers. It's dependent on safe workers.

Safe workers don't believe in luck. Instead, they believe their decisions and actions play huge roles in keeping safe.

Safety requires *wise decisions*.

Safety requires *wise actions*.

Being an Obedient Child to God: The Faith Factor

● Safety truth:

> *Being safe not only includes **prudent decisions** but also **protection**.*

As a beloved child of God, I've wonderfully discovered two immutable truths over the years of my life:

1. *Obedience to God* keeps you under the "umbrella" of His supreme protection, where you'll be safe from real dangers.
2. *Disobedience to God* leads you from under the "umbrella" of His supreme protection, where you'll be exposed to real dangers.

The real fact of the matter is that trusting in God to keep you safe won't do you much good if you're not *obeying Him*.

To obey God is to be an *obedient child* to God.

An obedient child to God is, first of all, *a child of God*.

To avoid any religious debate here, every person on earth is a child of God *by virtue of having been created by God*.

However, the Bible makes it very clear that there are two classes of children on earth: The children of God and the children of the devil.

> *In this the CHILDREN OF GOD are manifest, and the CHILDREN OF THE DEVIL: whosoever doeth not righteousness is not of God, neither he that loveth not his brother.*
>
> —1 JOHN 3:10

The person who receives God's Son, Jesus, as his or her personal Savior and Lord, is **adopted** *into the family of God*. "For ye are all the children of God BY FAITH IN CHRIST JESUS," (Galatians 3:26).

The family of God includes:

- The holy angels of God in heaven
- The soul-spirits of [human beings] in heaven [who died on earth, having received Jesus as their personal Savior and Lord]
- The people who've received Jesus as their personal Savior and Lord and are still alive on the earth, serving God in righteousness and living for Him . . . not themselves.

It's quite simple to determine *whose child you are.*
Whose child you are is either God or the devil.
God or the devil is your *spiritual parent.*
Your spiritual parent is *whose will* which you will do.
▶ God's will is that you lead a life of righteousness (doing what is morally right and spiritually pure) in His sight.
▶ The devil's will is that you lead a life of wickedness (doing what is morally bad or spiritually unclean) in his sight.

Whoever is your spiritual parent is who you will *obey.*
Who you will obey is whose will that you will do.
Look at your life. Ask yourself: *Whose will am I doing?*
Whose will you're doing belongs to God or the devil.
The answer to your question reveals your spiritual parent.

If you've received the Son of God, Jesus, as your personal Savior and Lord, then you're adopted into the family of God. You're a member of God's family . . . by faith.

As a member of God's family, you are *God's child.*

As God's child on earth, He expects you to reverence Him . . . as your Heavenly Father.

- ◈ To reverence Him is to obey Him . . . in all things.
- ◈ To reverence Him is to live to please Him . . . not your self.
- ◈ To reverence Him is to live how He wants you to live . . . not how you want to live . . . in this world.

If you haven't received the Son of God, Jesus, as your personal Savior and Lord, then you haven't been adopted into the family of God . . . which means you're still a member of the family of the devil.

You're yet an *unbeliever.*

The family of the devil includes:

- The evil angels (who follow him)
- The demons (which deceive and torment people . . . in all kinds of ways)
- All unbelievers—people in this world who don't believe on Jesus either as the Son of God or as their personal Savior and Lord

Simply put, you're either a child of God or a child of the devil. There is no third alternative. There is no third class of people to be in. You're either one or the other.

Just remember this significant difference between these two spiritual parents:

▶ God *loves* and diligently seeks to *protect* His child on earth.
▶ The devil *hates* and diligently seeks to *destroy* his child on earth.

God wants you to be safe . . . in the workplace . . . and He wants you to trust in Him as your Heavenly Father, to keep you safe.

The devil wants you to be unsafe . . . in the workplace . . . and he wants you to pull foolish stunts, to hopefully hurt yourself . . . if not to kill yourself.

The bottom line is this: The person, who's really a child of God and is really obedient to Him, can *trust in* God . . . and *truly expect* Him . . . to keep him or her safe and sound . . . virtually *anywhere in this world.*

Anywhere in this world can include *the workplace.*

God is not a "Superman" that the workplace could be "Kryptonite" to. His divine power . . . and supernatural abilities . . . cannot be weakened . . . not even by the real challenges and real dangers of the workplace. Amen!

Being "Fire Proof"

● Safety truth:

*A safe employee **works** safe because he **wants** to be safe.*

In this last chapter, I want to exhort and encourage you to trust in God to keep you safe and sound in the workplace . . . and practically anywhere in the world you may find yourself.

For this reason, I use Biblical examples of God's faithfulness to be the Personal Protection of them that put their trust in Him . . . to keep them safe and sound.

The plain facts of this case regarding workplace safety should ring loud and clear to you:

1. Your company [you work for] can only do so much to help keep you safe.
2. Your fellow workers can only do so much to help keep you safe.
3. You yourself can only do so much to keep yourself self.

All of these people mentioned above are *human beings*.
Human beings have *their limits*.
Having their limits, they're limited in what they can do . . . and that includes helping keep you safe.

There is a *Divine Being*.
That Divine Being is God.
God has *no limits*.
Having no limits, He's unlimited in what He can do. He's able to keep you safe exceeding abundantly above all of what you may ask or think.

God is the only One who can keep you safe from freak accidents.

Freak accidents are unpredictable. They catch people "totally off guard." They never "see" them coming. They "come out of the blue." They happen without warning.

Notwithstanding, what happened to three Hebrew children in particular, long ago was no freak accident.

The Bible tells the ancient story of a three young men of Hebrew descent, who were cast into a very real fiery furnace, to be burned alive for their "defiance," which was refusing to bow down and worship the golden image the Babylonian king had erected. Furious, the Babylonian king commanded they be bound and cast into the burning fiery furnace.

> *And he* [the Babylonian king] *commanded the most mighty men that were in his army to bind Shadrach, Meshach, and Abednego, and to cast them into the burning fiery furnace.*
>
> —DANIEL 3:20

These three young Hebrew men, led away in captivity from their homeland and brought to Babylon as slaves, trusted in God as their Personal Protection. As the king commanded, they were bound and cast into the burning fiery furnace. But because they trusted in God to protect them in their fiery ordeal, something incredible happened:

> *Then Nebuchadnezzar the king was astonished, and rose up in haste, and spake, and said unto his counselors, Did not we cast three men bound into the midst of the fire? They answered and said unto the king, True, O king. He answered and said, Lo, I see FOUR MEN loose, walking in the midst of the fire, and they have no hurt; AND THE FORM OF THE FOURTH IS LIKE THE SON OF GOD.*
>
> —DANIEL 3:24-25

These three Hebrew young men proved to be "fire proof" by their faith . . . their trust in God to keep them safe.

God will not only protect you from *freak accidents*.

He will also protect you from *evil intents*.

Evil intents are what evil people have against you, who don't like you or have a really big problem with you.

But hey, though people will be people, God will be God.

That's all that really matters.

In this sense, you can be "fire proof" in the workplace.

In the workplace, God can protect you from *literal* fires or *figurative* ones, which may jeopardize your very physical well-being.

Trust in Him to be your Personal Protection . . . especially in the workplace.

The workplace is home to many real dangers . . . some of which can be humanly guarded against . . . and some of which only God can guard against.

Being a "Miracle" . . . Instead of a "Meal"

● Safety truth:

> *Just as you have to keep your **fear** of what can harm you, you have to keep your **focus** on what you're doing.*

The Bible tells of another age-old story about yet another Hebrew man, whose name was Daniel.

Daniel also trusted in God as his Personal Protection. There came a day when as it was Daniel's custom (or habit) to pray that people who "had a problem with" him, wanted to see Daniel "get into trouble" . . . with the king. Charged with violation of the king's command concerning prayer, Daniel was cast into a den of lions.

> *Then the king commanded, and they brought Daniel, and cast him into the den of lions. Now the king spake and said unto Daniel, Thy God whom thou servest continually, HE WILL DELIVER THEE. And a stone was brought, and laid upon the mouth of the den; and the king sealed it with his own signet, and with the signets of his lords; that the purpose might not be changed concerning Daniel.*
>
> —DANEIL 6:16-17

The king arose very early in the morning to see if Daniel's God had, indeed, protected him . . . from the lions.

> *And when he came to the den, he cried with a lamentable voice unto Daniel: and the king spake and said unto Daniel, O Daniel, servant of the living God, is thy God, whom thou servest continually, able to deliver thee from the lions? Then said Daniel unto the king, O king, live for ever. My God hath sent His angel, and hath shut the lions' mouths, that they have not hurt me: forasmuch as before Him innocency was found in me; and also before thee, O king, have I done no hurt.*
>
> —DANIEL 6:20-22

God will be your Personal Protection . . . from what you cannot humanly possibly safeguard yourself against . . . if you will trust in Him to do so.

- Trust in God is *faith*.
- Faith requires *obedience* . . . to God, to be effectual.
- Obedience to God is *proof of love*.

In workplaces around the world, it's a miracle that many people are still alive, after being in very serious accidents on the job. I call these people who're very fortunate to have their lives, "miracles."

Don't let the workplace be a "den of lions," where as lions, incidents will "feed on" you.

You stand by faith . . . in the workplace.

The workplace cannot lock out God's presence and power.

God appears *anywhere on earth* He so chooses.

▶ The earth is His material creation.

▶ The people that populate the earth are His human creation.

The God of *power* is also the God of *preservation*.

He will preserve you . . . from day to day . . . from workday to workday . . . as you trust in Him to do so.

Faith pleases Him . . . not *foolishness*.

He expects you to do the right thing, the safe thing, *continually*.

Here are some key observations I made regarding Daniel's lions'-den experience:

1. God will assign *protective angels* to you.

2. Your *faith* (trust in God) is the key to your supernatural protection.
3. Your *obedience* is the key requirement for your faith to produce the desired result.
4. Your trust in God . . . to keep you safe . . . will give you *blessed assurance*. You can work in peace or without being worried about getting hurt . . . or killed.
5. Trust in God makes you *confident* . . . not *overconfident*.
6. Daniel didn't do any thing wrong to deserve being thrown into a den of lions. You must not do any thing you well know will get you hurt or killed. Don't foolishly force tests on God. He doesn't have to try to "pass" them. Always take the safe way . . . of doing things.
7. Even if God doesn't *prevent* an incident from taking place, He is still well able to *protect* you in it.
8. As His dear child, God is never *against* you; only *for you*.

Your life is yours to live . . . and to offer to God as a pleasing sacrifice . . . to serve Him and live like He wants you to.

His supreme protection hinges on that.

Whatever you may choose to do in life, make sure it doesn't threaten your physical well-being or endanger your very life.

Stay on the safe path.

Make the right decisions . . . in the workplace.

Trust in God to be your Personal Protection.

Believe He's not in the business of failing to safeguard His beloved children in this world, as they put their unflinching trust in Him.

Being a "Faith Giant" . . .
Instead of a "Foolishly Self-confident Giant"

● Safety truth:

Safety requires your **commitment** *to it . . . and your* **continual observance** *of it.*

Another classical example of the Bible, of God's faithfulness to be the Personal Protection of the person who trusts in Him, is the famous story of David and Goliath.

Basically, it was a *battle between two giants*.

▶ Goliath was a *foolishly self-confident giant*. He trusted in himself, to protect himself.

▶ David was a *faith giant*. He trusted in God to protect him.

The one who was foolishly self-confident, who trusted in himself, lost the battle to the other, who was wisely confident in God and trusted in God.

Goliath lost the battle to David.

David was *supernaturally protected . . . by God*.

God honored David's complete trust in Him . . . to protect him from the Philistine giant.

⬇ The multitude of onlookers considered David to be the *underdog*.
⬇ The Mighty God considered David to be the *undisputed champion*.

It is always wise to trust in God to keep you safe, and not yourself.

Yes, you have your part to do, in keeping safe. But there's a grave difference between being foolishly self-confident and being faithful . . . or full of faith (trust in God).

Here are some key observations I made in the story of David and Goliath:

1. People who are *arrogant* think . . . and feel . . . they don't need God. Rather, they think they're self-sufficient . . . to take care of themselves.
2. People who think they're *self-sufficient* rely on their *strength*. But their strength has a limit. They have limited abilities. Even their very intelligence is limited.
3. People, who are proud, are prone to trust in themselves. Humble people have a natural inclination to trust in God.
4. The size of your *problem* should be matched by the size of your *faith*. Goliath was a giant problem for the Israelite nation. Fortunately, among them was found a man of giant faith.
5. Safe workers are *ordinary* people, who can trust in an *extraordinary* God, to be their Personal Protection.

6. When answering challenges . . . or difficult tasks . . . trust in God to *help* you, and to keep you from *hurting* yourself . . . and your chance for promotion.

Be confident in God and take courage against the "Goliaths" or giant problems in regard to safety that you may find in your workplace.

Through your trust in God, defeat:

- The "giant" of *distraction* . . . *by people and/or things*
- The "giant" of *violation* . . . *of safety rules*
- The "giant" of *rebellion* . . . *against the will of the company*
- The "giant" of *mental preoccupation* . . . *by personal/family problems*
- The "giant" of *determination* . . . *to get the job done*

These are giant problems found in the workplace, especially steel mills. But, you don't have to be *victimized* by these "giants." Instead, you can be *victorious* over them . . . by your commitment to doing things the safest way you know how and trusting in God to safeguard you from what you cannot possibly safeguard yourself.

The I.C.E. S.H.I.E.L.D.
That Protects the Safe Workplace

● Safety truth:

> *Safety essentially requires focus, which is a* **power** *of the mind you should make your* **practice.**

Using the words *ICE SHIELD* as acronyms, I let each letter stand for the following:

Instructing
Common
Employees

Safe
Habits (for)

Individual
Employees (to)
Learn (and)
Develop

Learning is a never-ending process.
You can always learn *something new.*
Something new is something *you didn't know.*
When you learn something you didn't know, you increase your knowledge.
You need to continually increase your safety knowledge.

Here are some safe habits for individual employees to learn and develop; for, it is safe habits that basically form the protective shield around a safe workplace. A safe workplace consists of safe workers.

Safe workers have learned and developed safe habits, and they keep an open mind to new possibilities and new ways of being safe . . . and even safer.

As I said earlier, when you trust in God to keep you safe, He *expects* you to "do your part," or do what you can do, to be safe. He created you with *common sense* . . . and He *expects* you to use it . . . continually. Learning and developing these safety habits will help you to "do your part," in keeping yourself safe.

Safe Habit #1: Always regard being in the workplace as being in a *dangerous place.* A dangerous place should naturally heighten your awareness of your surroundings and amplify your fear of what's in it that can potentially harm you. A dangerous place is not a place to relax your vigilance or retire your respect for what can hurt or kill you.

Safe Habit #2: Always abide by what I call the *law of inspection.* Always inspect your work area, machinery, and tools before starting up. Go a second mile with your safety by conducting periodic checks of these things . . . throughout your work shift. Your work shift has a time limit. That time limit is a certain *amount of time.* Anything is subject to happen in that amount of time. Respect the possibility of what *could happen.*

Safe Habit #3: Always respect the fact that though machines are made to serve you, they're *monsters* in the real sense they can harm you . . . and frighten your family and friends, who don't want anything bad to happen to you. *Machines are subject to malfunction.* Malfunction can occur in a moment. Every moment must be spent being safe.

Safe Habit #4: Always respect the dangerous potential and power of little things. Little things can seem very harmless, but it's often the little things that get workers. Workers need to learn to respect the little things and not make light of them, to treat them as minor concerns. A tree grows from a seed. Something major can "grow from" something minor. A simple cut or scrape or scratch can lead to infection, if not attended to. Infection can lead to a grave situation.

Safe Habit #5: Always fear shortcuts . . . when they're unsafe to take. The moment you decide to take a shortcut is the same moment you decide to put yourself at risk. A shortcut is a seed from which a serious incident can grow. Shortcuts can be *dangerous routes* to arriving at completion of your tasks. Oftentimes, the *long way* of doing things is the safe way to take. A safe worker takes the safe way . . . of doing things.

Safe Habit #6: Always communicate. Communication is a success key to teamwork. Teamwork is an ultimate necessity for having a safe workplace. Teamwork involves more than working together to get the job done. It is also helping one another to keep safe. Communication keeps you "in touch" with one another. Being "out of touch" with fellow workers is never good. Learn to make known to them your intents, your situation, your need for help, etc. *Don't expect them to be mind-readers.*

Safe Habit #7: Always be mentally alert. Mental alertness is the secret to staying focused. Staying focused is a personal task which you must fulfill throughout the entirety of your work shift. Your mind is a *tool* and it has the *task* of processing information and interpreting situations and events. Your mind plays a crucial role in getting through the workday safe and sound. *If your mind isn't "there" or on what you're doing, you're no more than a walking zombie in the workplace.* A "work zombie" can be subject to a zillion incidents. That worker will have far more than enough opportunities to get hurt.

Safe Habit #8: Always wear *all* of your personal protective equipment. Armor is no good to a warrior who doesn't have it on. Wearing your PPE is one of the most important things you can do to keep yourself safe. No one else can wear it *for you*. You have to wear it for *yourself*. It is a personal responsibility. It is the mark of a responsible worker. It is an automatic indication that you don't want to get hurt. Remember: Do what you can do, and trust God to do what you cannot do, in keeping safe.

Safe Habit #9: Always think before you act. Think about what you're going to do *before* you do it. *Analyze you actions.* Consider the consequences. Examine before you execute. *Unsafe actions are seeds for incidents.* Learn to allot your time in the workplace wisely. Some of your time should be allotted to consideration. Your work should not be entirely comprised of action. You're not just a worker. You're also a *thinker. THINK!*

Safe Habit #10: Always ask about what you're unsure or uncertain of. *Pride can prove to be a killer.* Assumption should be a forbidden practice to you. *Ignorance can be a seed for an incident. If you don't know, then don't go forward . . . with what you intended to do!* Stop. Seek advice or guidance. Recognize your need for others. The workplace is not for a one-man show. It is for full utilization of the teamwork concept.

Safe Habit #11: Always corral your negative emotions. Take control of how you feel. Negative emotions, such as anger, bitterness, disappointment, etc, can blind you to being safe. They can impede your focus. They can hinder your mental alertness. They can dangerously claim your undivided attention. Don't let a negative emotion cause commotion in the "world" of your heart. Your heart must be kept uncluttered. *Feelings affect your focus.* Your focus is key to keeping safe.

Learn and develop these safe habits.
Safe habits form the protective shield around a safe workplace.
I call this protective shield around a safe workplace the I.C.E. S.H.I.E.L.D.
Therefore when workers put away their safe habits, they, in essence, destroy the I.C.E. S.H.I.E.L.D. that protects the workplace.
Always honor the safe habits you've learned and developed, and thereby help preserve the I.C.E. S.H.I.E.L.D. that surrounds and protects your workplace.

To the Safety-Talker:
The Message That Makes a Difference

● Safety truth:

> *Safety should not only be a **vision** but also it should be given a **voice**.*

James 1:5 states:

> *If any of you lack wisdom, let him ask of God, that giveth to all men liberally, and upbraideth not; and it shall be given him.*

A safety-talker gives safety talks.

Safety talks should be messages that make a difference.

For this very reason, I exhort the safety-talker to *pray for a wise message*.

A wise message (on safety, of course) has four success principles to it. Let's identify them:

1. A safety talk should be a *live* one. Dead talks don't do much to encourage and inspire anyone. An uninspired audience is the proof of a failed safety talk. *Inspiration is an indication of a successful safety talk.* God can give you a message that will be full of life! Such a message will captivate your audience and hold their undivided attention, as it innocently yet powerfully draws them into itself. The safety-talker should not be boring . . . but brilliantly interesting.
2. A safety talk should be an *effective* one. It should have an intended or expected effect on the audience. The audience should leave *changed . . . not the same*. People should leave with an even greater appreciation for safety and the tools they're given, to help build a safe environment. The safety-talker should not be merely a filler of time but a fantastic speaker to listen to.
3. A safety talk should be a *sharp* one. It should be intellectually penetrating. It should "pierce" the heart of every person listening . . . intently . . . and "cut through" all the "layers" of reasoning people may have, regarding keeping safe, which may

not really be appropriate. The safety-talker should not be merely a messenger but a mighty deliverer of a safety talk that gets right to the "core issues" of safety with people.
4. A safety talk should be a *perceptive* one. It should *reveal* to people the unsafe things of the heart they may have thought or intended to do, and *redirect* them to do things the safe way. The safety-talker should not only be a common realist but also an uncommon revolutionist . . . to advocate change of methods and change of hearts; to reach out to every single person in the audience and persuade him or her to do the right thing . . . when they leave out and return to their work area or return home.

The message that makes a difference may save someone's life. Don't take a safety talk for granted.

A safety talk should always be purposefully designed as a *key*, to unlock one more way of keeping safe.

The safety-talker should see himself . . . or herself . . . as a *key master*. He or she should always seek to give people keys to keeping safe; and, they should always remember that God can . . . and will . . . give to them keys of knowledge . . . on workplace safety . . . if they ask Him for it. *Research* is one thing. *Revelation* is another.

5 Beautiful Types of Safety-Talkers

1. **"Ambassadors."** These are the most prominent safety-talkers. They hold high positions within the company. I refer to them as "ambassadors" because they know the mind and heart of the company and therefore understand the company's intentions and purposes in workplace safety. They have a firm grasp of the "big picture" the company has of safety for its divisions. Because they know the mind of the company on workplace safety, they can think with the mind of the company on workplace safety, to establish the same mindset of the company in the workplaces of its respective divisions. They visit different divisions of the company they represent, to establish safe workplaces.
2. **"Messengers."** These are the "spokespersons" for the company. I refer to them as "messengers" because they speak for the company

that may "hire" them, to speak from their own fields of work, in terms of being safe. The company may have such people as police officers, firefighters, doctors, nurses, and the like, to conduct safety talks. They interpret the company's will on workplace safety to the workers. The company may "send them out," to deliver messages to the people directly from the company, which honors what the company has done to bring the workers to where they are and call forth new possibilities to move them to a new place.

3. **"Safety violator winners."** These are the safety-talkers whose main concern is winning safety violators over to abandoning their unsafe practices and adopting safe practices. Their safety talks concentrate on the real issue of safety violation, the causes and consequences of it, and exhortation and encouragement to do the right things and take the safe ways. They guide workers into the safe practices that both characterize and nurture the ideally safe workplace.

4. **"Feeders."** These are safety-talkers who are "married to" their respective workplace. The very place where they work is the place they're willing to do safety talks. They seem to have a passion for "feeding" fellow workers all kinds of information . . . from incidents to instructions and insights. Research plays a major role in composing their safety talks. Like a shepherd who cares for his sheep, they have a genuine concern for their fellow workers, to be safe.

5. **"Teachers."** These are safety-talkers who seek to condition workers to a certain action or frame of mind. I refer to them as "teachers" because their safety talks are purposefully designed to impart knowledge to the workers. These safety-talkers communicate and interpret the meaning of Safety and what it means to be safe. They seek to understand, interpret, and explain general subjects on safety. They bring a sense of balance to the safety effort of the company.

Over the years, I have carefully observed and correctly identified these five beautiful types of safety-talkers. I consider them real blessings to the workers . . . and to the safety efforts of the company. Their safety talks respectively are geared at making you the utmost possible safest worker you can be. So learn to genuinely appreciate them and listen intently to them whenever they conduct safety talks. As bullets that need guns to deliver them and arrows that need bows to deliver them, safety talks need safety-talkers to deliver them. Safety-talkers are for your sake!

An H.A.P.P.Y. Ending

● Safety truth:

> *An employee has his **reason** [or excuse] for his safety violation just as he has his **reaction** to the punishment he incurs.*

I wrote this book on workplace safety with *YOU in mind.*
I want you to be the best possible safest worker you can be.
If that weren't enough, I want you to trust in God to keep you safe, as you do your part to keep yourself safe . . . no matter where in this world you may find yourself.

Using the word *HAPPY* as an acronym, I let each letter stand for the following:

Humble
Affirmative
Prayer (for)
Protection (for)
You

I want every single one of your workdays to have what I call an H.A.P.P.Y. ending.
I want you to believe God to keep you safe from day to day . . . from workday to workday . . . as you live your life, seeking to please Him in all things.

Here is a humble, affirmative prayer for protection I've composed for you, which you can pray every single day. Just as the *world* can be a dangerous place to live in, the *workplace* can be a dangerous place to work in.

Heavenly Father,

I thank You for this day. I thank You for this new mercy I see. I believe You will be a shield to them that trust in You . . . to protect them . . . to keep them safe. I trust in You to be my Personal Protection, as You were the

Personal Protection of those three Hebrew young men in the fiery furnace; and just as You were the Personal Protection of Daniel in the lions' den. You are the same yesterday, today, and forever. You change not. You are no respecter of persons. What You did for them I believe . . . and trust . . . You to do for me. I thank You that no weapon formed against me . . . in the world or in the workplace . . . shall prosper. I thank You for protecting me from all unseen dangers and hidden traps. I thank You for protecting me from freak accidents, and from the sabotage of mean men with evil intent against me. If I have any unsafe way of doing anything, I ask You, in the multitude of Your mercy, to reveal to me that I may repent of it. No one in this whole world can keep me like You can. I thank You for keeping me as the apple of Your eye this blessed day, in Jesus' name. Amen.

SAFETY COUNSEL FOR YOU TO CONSIDER

- *Frustration* can be the *fraction* of your focus. Broken focus is a seed for an incident.
- When it comes to being the safest worker you can be, *diligent effort* is insufficient. You also require *divine intervention.*
- To *ignore* safety rules and regulations is to *invite* incidents . . . to happen.
- The unsafe practice you're unwilling to *release* is the same one you'll *regret.*
- The crowning reward for *being safe* is *being alive.*
- Workplace safety is a *personal responsibility* . . . and a *prayer request.*
- Your *health* is a major part of your *happiness.* Unsafe conduct can damage/diminish your health.
- Having a *proper attitude* towards safety is as important as having *protective angels.*
- *Foolish stunts* can be open invitations for *fatal accidents.*
- Safe workers are *mature* . . . not *mischievous.*
- Dangerous conditions should be *recognized* . . . and *respected.*
- If you don't consider *Safety's voice,* you will commit *safety violation.*
- When you *love* yourself you'll *look to be* safe . . . in all your ways, in the workplace.

Epilogue

My Seven Year Itch

On a cold, December day in 2006, pondering the steady decline and uncertain future of my place of employment, I didn't want to wait to see what would happen in the days to come. All I could see was a sinking ship I wisely needed to abandon, before I went down with it. Mustering up the courage, I set my sights on a new place of employment . . . a steel mill.

For common courtesy's sake, I put in my two-week notice.

Though my supervisor . . . and many others . . . didn't want to see me leave, they understood it was imperative I did. Some condemned me. Others commended me. Irregardless, my mind was made up . . . to move on.

On Friday, February 2, 2007, I stopped working at my old job; and, on the following Monday, February 5, 2007, I started working at my new job. The transition went smoothly for me, for which I was very grateful.

Seeing immediately Safety was this company's highest priority, I said to myself,

> *"If I work here that long, I'm going to give it a period of seven years, to see what I can discover about workplace safety. I'll carefully observe my new place of employment, to see what perceptions I can have, what discoveries I can make, what lessons I can learn, in regard to safety. I will keep silent about my discoveries. I will not reveal my discovered secrets. I will honor this*

self-imposed commitment, to ensure I have good understanding of the things whereof I may affirm."

So, for seven secret years of silence, I held my peace.

At the fulfillment of seven years of employment, I set myself to publish my findings in a book.

Within that precise timeframe—from February 5, 2007 to February 5, 2014—I diligently labored, to glean every possible, precious nugget of knowledge of workplace safety.

At the conclusion of my seven-year period of silence, during which I itched to share my wonderful findings, I rejoiced in spirit when the long-awaited time finally came for me to become a joyous revealer of the marvelous secrets I'd patiently learned, passionately lived, and powerfully led.

People were precious to me. The human body was an amazing work of art, wrought by the most cunning hand of God, the Blessed Creator of us all. Human life was dear. The very thought of people getting hurt or killed in the workplace (where they worked to support their families and themselves) ached my heart.

Then I saw and well did I consider. Looking upon the workplace, I received valuable insight:

> *The workplace is a **real money-making place**, but also can be a **real monster**. Respect it to remain alive.*

I sincerely hope this book, born out of the fiery ashes of my workplace experiences over the years, will be a burning light, to show others the grave importance of working safe and the true hope of being safe.

I pray the Wonderful Wisdom of this book . . . on workplace safety . . . find its way into the hearts and minds of many, who work for a living or have others working for them.

In the final analysis, this have I learned: Though work is a necessity, safety is a noble responsibility.

God bless . . .

—L. A. Jones